PRUNING MADE EASY

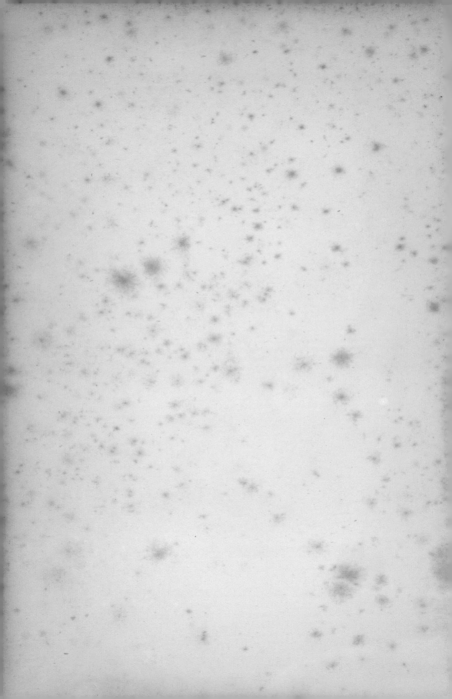

One of the very best Roses for amateurs, ''Lady Pirrie.'' It blooms freely in summer and autumn; the flowers are of salmon-red shade

PRUNING MADE EASY

How to Prune Rose Trees, Fruit Trees and Ornamental Trees and Shrubs

Edited by
H. H. THOMAS
(Editor of " Popular Gardening ")

Illustrated by eight full page Plates from photographs and numerous diagrams in the text

CASSELL AND COMPANY, LTD.
London, Toronto, Melbourne and Sydney

First Edition *January* 1927
Second   „   *March*   1941

PREFACE

In every garden there are rose trees, fruit trees, or ornamental trees and shrubs, that need to be pruned annually, and the amateur is often at a loss to know how to proceed. Frequently he trims the trees without being at all sure whether he is doing the right thing. He is faced with the difficulty that trees need pruning at different seasons of the year, some must be cut back or thinned out, while others ought scarcely to be pruned at all.

It is little wonder that he is bewildered and seeks refuge in a general tidying up, in the spring of the year, by cutting back all branches that seem in the way. Yet, as a perusal of this book will show, it is an easy matter to understand the principles that underlie the pruning of trees and shrubs; this practice is governed chiefly by the season at which they bloom. If he knows that, the amateur will soon realise why certain kinds are pruned in spring, others in summer, and so on. But if he proceeds in haphazard fashion and contents himself with a general trimming in autumn or spring, he is certain to spoil the display of some kinds and will fail to get the best from others.

This volume is separated into three parts which deal respectively with the pruning of roses, fruit trees, and ornamental trees and shrubs. Mr. A. Osborn has written the notes dealing with ornamental trees and shrubs, Mr. B. W. Price has contributed the chapter on "Prune these Roses Lightly," and two or three of the chapters on pruning fruit trees are by Mr. J. Townend.

H. H. T.

CONTENTS

PART I—PRUNING ROSE TREES

PART II—PRUNING FRUIT TREES

PART III—PRUNING TREES AND SHRUBS

APPENDIX

LIST OF ILLUSTRATIONS

Full Page Plates

Diagrams in the Text

PRUNING MADE EASY

PART I

PRUNING ROSE TREES

CHAPTER I

A Chat about Pruning

MANY rose-growers have their own theories on the subject of pruning, and when in their own gardens those theories are put to the test and yield results that are satisfactory there is a likelihood that they may be broadcast and recommended to all and sundry. No doubt, in due course, methods of rose-tree pruning that are generally practised at the present time will become obsolete and will be replaced by others as the result of continued experiment, and in part will have been forced upon us by new types of roses. If we compare the methods of pruning rose trees now found most suitable with those that were deemed best a generation ago, considerable differences will be discerned—differences that are due chiefly to the fact that the roses themselves exhibit greater variety in habit of growth.

The truth is that rose-tree pruning, like all other gardening "operations," must progress with the times : if we continue to lay down hard and fast rules and to make dogmatic assertions that brook no contradiction, sooner or later we shall find ourselves out of date in our recommendations, we shall realise that we have not kept pace with our subject.

It is absurd to imagine that one can say, "Cut this branch here and that branch there, cut this shoot in March and that shoot in July," and in other stereotyped ways reduce the subject of pruning to something resembling a mathematical formula. Such information may be helpful to those who take no real interest in gardening and like to have a presentable show of bloom with as little trouble as possible, but it can never prove a reliable guide that will enable the keen grower to obtain the best results from his trees.

First Considerations

Rules there must be if a book on the subject is to be helpful, but if the reader follows them slavishly without exercising common sense and using his powers of observation, and if he treats all his trees alike, then he will succeed with some and will as certainly fail with others.

To get the very best from one's rose trees it is necessary to take into account first of all the variety of rose being dealt with, for modern rose trees vary greatly in the way in which they grow. Some are of stiff, upright growth, others have slender, spreading branches, some are vigorous, others are weakly. Then one has also to consider the climatic and other conditions in which the roses are grown and the health of the trees themselves; they may be thriving lustily or they may be weakly and lacking in vigour; obviously the trees must benefit by careful consideration of their individual needs.

The whole subject is full of perplexities, some of which the amateur can solve only by studying his plants and taking note of the way in which they respond to, or are affected by, different methods of treatment. Perhaps the most helpful way of treating the matter is first to describe the orthodox methods of pruning and then to discuss such variations of them as have been recommended and practised by growers who have carried out experiments.

Rule-of-Thumb Methods

There is this to be said for the ways of pruning rose trees that are generally followed—they have been evolved after years of experience and practice and have been found to yield satisfactory results generally. Although they may have been handed down from one generation of gardeners to another, and accepted without demur and without critical examination, and so far may be regarded as rule-of-thumb methods, it is nevertheless true that they would scarcely have found favour for so long if they had not yielded tolerably good results.

New Roses—New Ways of Pruning

The doubts that have been cast on these orthodox methods during the last few years have arisen because of the different kinds of rose trees with which we have to deal. Roses cannot be grown to perfection merely by applying the usual rules of pruning that have been

recommended for years. Those ways are sound enough
but they must be varied according to the type and variety
dealt with, and there, in a nutshell, you have the whole
secret of successful pruning. As has been pointed out,
the trees vary greatly and it does not follow that because
one variety thrives when pruned in a particular way
that another will do so.

CHAPTER II

Why we Prune Rose Trees

WHY do we prune rose trees? Why not let them grow as they will, as we do with many other shrubs? As a matter of fact some rose trees are all the better for little or no pruning, but of that more anon.

When roses are planted in flower beds of limited size and in gardens of restricted area it becomes necessary to restrain and direct their growth for the purposes of keeping the bushes shapely and the garden orderly and to ensure the production of blooms of fair size and quality. It may thus be said that the objects of pruning rose trees are to keep them within reasonable bounds, of shapely form, and to get rid of useless branches, so strengthening those that remain that they will bear satisfactory blooms.

If left unpruned, most rose trees, at all events those varieties commonly grown for filling formal flower beds, would become straggling, untidy, bare at the base, and their development would be hindered by the presence of thin weakly shoots that are in themselves useless and disadvantageous to the others : further, the blooms, though numerous, would probably be lacking in size and form or shapeliness.

The way in which we cultivate rose trees is artificial, and we must continue to practise artificial methods in our

5

management of them. If we had unlimited room for rose-growing and could allow each bush to develop to its utmost extent, merely thinning out old and weakly branches,we should achieve astonishing results with certain varieties, but, as matters are, if we wish to grow a representative selection in a restricted space they must be kept within bounds by pruning or cutting back the branches.

Easily Grown Roses

It is as well to realise that a rose tree can be grown to perfection without being pruned in the orthodox way. One has only to take note of giant bushes in the gardens of those people who like to have roses in bloom but have no real interest in them or in other details of garden work; all the pruning they do is to trim back the tips of the branches in spring and to cut out dead shoots. Yet the results they achieve are often of astonishing excellence; the bushes grow vigorously and bloom profusely, though the flowers are usually more remarkable for quantity than quality. It must be added that the roses planted by such folk are limited to a few vigorous varieties that resent hard pruning, such as Hugh Dickson, Frau Karl Druschki, and Caroline Testout, which are almost certain to succeed under those conditions. It is, however, probable that many other roses would do equally well if more lightly pruned than is usual.

By pruning a rose tree we make it conform to the object we have in view. If we prune the branches severely

The rambler Roses provide a blaze of bloom in summer—
"Blush Rambler" trained over a tall pole

each spring we shall have a comparatively low bush that will yield blooms of the largest size and the best shape that particular variety can produce. If, on the other hand, we prune the branches lightly or scarcely at all we shall obtain a bigger and less shapely bush bearing more numerous flowers probably lacking in size and beauty of form.

CHAPTER III

General Instructions

WHEN ought rose trees to be pruned? From the end of March to the middle of April is the usual time to prune bushes or dwarfs. Rambler rose trees should be pruned in late summer or as soon as the flower display is over. Climbing, as distinct from rambler, roses should be pruned in autumn and looked over again in spring. At the autumn pruning of rambler and climbing roses such old branches or parts of them as can be replaced by fresh shoots should be cut out. In spring the only pruning to be done is to cut off the soft or damaged ends of the branches and to shorten the side shoots on the old branches that remain—the side shoots are cut back to two or three buds.

Those who live in the colder districts of the country are well advised to prune their bush roses during the first three weeks of April, the Tea varieties being left until the last. In milder districts the hybrid perpetual roses, such as Ulrich Brunner, Frau Karl Druschki, Mrs. John Laing, and Captain Hayward, may be pruned towards the end of March; the Hybrid Teas, such as Ophelia and General McArthur, the first week in April; and the Teas—Madame Antoine Mari, A. Hill Gray, and Marie Van Houtte—for instance, the second or third week in the month.

Merely taking off the tops is not the right treatment for a Bush Rose tree.

How a Bush Rose tree should look after pruning is completed

The top bud on pruned shoots should point outward as shown.

B

The earlier the rose trees are pruned the sooner will they bloom. If they are pruned lightly they will flower earlier than if pruned severely. To have roses in full bloom in June, light pruning is necessary; if they are to be at their best in July hard pruning is required.

It is a mistake to prune rose bushes earlier than at the times named. The earlier they are pruned the sooner will they start to make fresh growth, and in the event of frosts late in April or early in May the new shoots are

Always cut close to a bud : if a " snag " is left it will die-back

liable to be damaged and the first display of bloom may be spoilt. If most of the pruning is carried out during the first fortnight in April the fresh shoots generally make uninterrupted progress.

Summer pruning is an important detail. This is practised continuously during the summer months and consists in shortening the shoots that have flowered. It is not enough merely to pick off the faded blooms, the shoot or branch ought also to be shortened by cutting at least three or four inches off the top. This will induce the bush to make fresh and vigorous shoots which in turn will yield a later supply of bloom.

Summer Pruning

Many modern roses continue to bloom more or less throughout the summer months, and as the blooms fade the shoots ought to be pruned back a few inches, the longest can be shortened by as much as six inches. They must not, of course, be cut back anywhere near the base, otherwise the lowest buds, which will produce the following year's flowering shoots, will start to grow and the "wood" they produce will not be of such good quality as the original shoot and it may not become thoroughly "ripened."

An Important Point

One of the most important points the amateur must bear in mind when pruning his rose trees is this : it is only the growth of the previous summer that is pruned, not the older, woody branches. Therefore when the advice given is to "prune to within four buds of the base" it is the base of the last summer's growth that is meant, not the base of the bush. It is necessary to make this point clear, because I have known beginners cut the branches of their rose trees almost to the ground level instead of merely pruning the past summer's shoots.

The ideal rose bush is one in which a limited number of branches, say five or six, grow in an outward direction and from which all dead and weakly shoots have been cut away. Having got rid of all useless shoots, the next thing to do is to cut the remaining ones to a bud that points away from the centre so that the ensuing shoot will grow in an outward direction, thus keeping the middle of the bush open.

The cut ought to be made immediately above a bud and in a slanting direction; it should begin just above the top of the bud on the same side of the shoot. After having made the cut it is wise to dress it with styptic or painter's knotting to prevent damage by the maggots of the pith-boring moth.

Prune to Sound Wood

One often sees rose bushes pruned in such a way that they will be full of snags or pieces of dead wood in summer. Instead of the shoot being cut off level with the top of the bud it is cut an inch or more above it; this part of the branch dies and the snag remains.

After a severe winter rose bushes may suffer a good deal of damage which may not be apparent on a superficial examination. For this reason it is always wise when cutting back a branch to look at the pith. If this is black or dark brown the branch is certain to die back beyond it. Pruning must be to a point at which the pith is not discoloured. This may lead to the branches being pruned more severely than was intended, but that is unavoidable; it is essential to cut back to what the rosarian calls "sound wood." If that is not done at pruning time in spring it will become necessary later in the season when the branch has died back to that point.

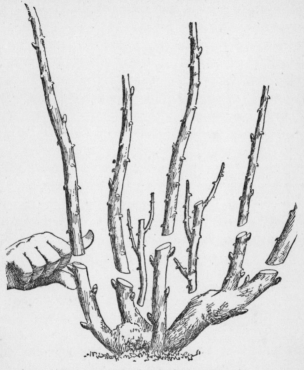

Prune to a bud pointing outwards

The pruning tools required are a saw for the removal of thick, hard, and old branches and a pair of secateurs or a pruning knife. Most rosarians use the secateurs nowadays in preference to a knife. The work can be done as well with that tool and far more expeditiously. It is worth while buying a really good pair of secateurs, for with care they will last for years and do their work well. Needless to say they ought to be sharp. If the shoots are cut with a blunt pair of secateurs or a blunt knife they will be bruised and that may cause them to die back. A clean cut can be made only with a sharp instrument.

While the shoot or branch is being cut with the right hand it ought to be held firmly with the left hand, otherwise there is a danger of its breaking off at some point lower down and possibly at the base. Some varieties of roses are very prickly, the stems being armed with strong, sharp spines. For this reason it is wise to wear a pair of gloves while pruning. Very thick gloves are not very convenient, for they interfere with the use of the pruning tool, but they must be made of strong material through which the spines will not penetrate easily.

CHAPTER IV

Pruning Dwarf or Bush Rose Trees

LET us first clearly understand what is meant by a dwarf or bush rose tree. It is so called to distinguish it from a standard or climbing rose; the bud is inserted on the stock close to the ground, and the height to which the plant grows depends on the vigour of the variety. The rose bush may reach a height of 2 feet or even less, or it may be 3 feet, 4 feet, or 5 feet high, according to the growth of the particular rose and the kind of pruning practised. But whatever height the tree reaches, it is still known technically as a dwarf or bush because the bud from which the whole plant develops was inserted low down near the ground level. In a standard rose the bud is inserted at the top of a stem that varies in height from 2 to 2½ feet to 3 or 4 feet, or even 5 feet in weeping standards.

The first thing to do in pruning a bush or dwarf rose tree is to cut out all dead or decaying shoots or branches; they affect the health of the tree adversely. The next thing is to prune away all very weakly shoots, those that tend to crowd the centre of the bush, thus hindering the development of stronger branches, and are in themselves useless because they are not strong enough to bloom.

These details having been attended to we have then

Spring planted
Roses should be pruned
to within 2 or 3 buds of the base
to make them break strongly

The cuts
need making
properly,

Cut
leaving
snag   W

Cut
injuring
bud

W

Too
horizon-
tal   W

Wrong
direct-
ion of
cut.

Right

A well sharpened knife,
is essential for making
clean pruning cuts.

to deal with a bush that possesses a limited number of branches varying in vigour according to the variety of rose in question. Some will be as thick as one's little finger, others no thicker than a lead pencil. The problem to be solved is to what extent these remaining branches are to be shortened, and that depends on the object in view and the characteristics of the variety.

Orthodox Way of Pruning

Let us take first the orthodox method of pruning to be recommended when the purpose is to provide a generous supply of flowers of fair size and quality that will make a good display in the garden. The shoots or branches are cut back to varying heights according to their vigour, the strong ones being pruned more lightly than the weak ones. Good general advice is to shorten the strongest to within from four to six buds of the base of the previous summer's growth, those rather less vigorous to three or four buds, and the weakest to one or two buds. If those instructions are carried out and the advice previously given in the chapter on General Instructions is followed the results are likely to be satisfactory. Before starting the work of pruning it is advisable that the reader should study Chapter V; if his collection includes varieties mentioned there he will be well advised to act accordingly.

There may be among the roses some of extra vigorous growth that are best suited by the pegging down method advocated in Chapter VI, but only those of unusual vigour can be dealt with in this way. The advice given above

An old Rose bush hard pruned to force fresh growth

applies to most of the decorative or garden roses in
general cultivation at the present time; most of them
belong to the Hybrid Tea class, familiar representatives
of which are Ophelia, Madame Leon Pain, Etoile de
Hollande, and General McArthur.

Now let us consider some of the variations from the
orthodox method that are recommended from time to
time. It is said by some rosarians that the usual method
of pruning rose bushes is too drastic, that it is a mistake
to cut away so much growth from the bushes annually,
and that they would develop into finer specimens, yield-
ing a greater number of blossoms, if pruned more lightly.
It is difficult to give a decided opinion on this matter, for
the growth of rose trees varies so greatly in different

varieties, in different localities, and according to the kind of soil in which they are planted. The beginner who likes to ensure a fair quantity of blooms can scarcely do better than follow the advice given already in this chapter, but if he is of an experimental turn of mind then he should practise different methods and take note of the result. Some varieties will respond to light pruning better than others. It is entirely a matter for experiment in the reader's own garden, for it does not

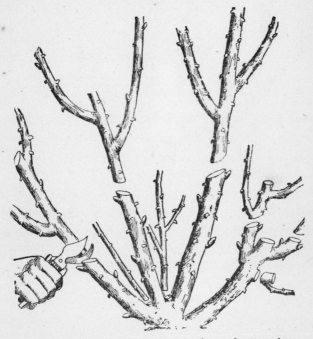

Thin shoots are cut out and others shortened

follow that a rose which in one garden grows into a large bush if very lightly pruned will do the same in another. It is safe as a rule to prune a bush lightly if it makes vigorous growth.

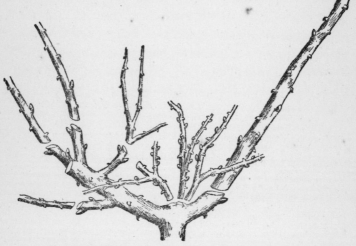

Pruning a Rose tree that has one strong shoot

When rose bushes are grown in formal beds on a lawn, for example, it is necessary to adopt a uniform system of pruning otherwise the rose beds would contain bushes of various sizes and their appearance would be spoilt. In planting a formal rose garden it is wise to fill each bed with one variety and to prune them on orthodox lines, shortening the previous summer's branches to within from one or two buds to five or six buds, according to whether they are weak or vigorous.

In the following lists an attempt has been made to classify some of the most popular of present-day roses according to the kind of pruning they need in the average garden.

Special Instructions

The following varieties are best dealt with by cutting out all thin, weakly shoots, pegging down the vigorous branches of four or five feet in length, and shortening those slightly less vigorous by one half or so :—

Avoca.

Clio.

Frau Karl Druschki.

George Dickson.

Hugh Dickson.

J. B. Clark.

H. E. Richardson.

La Tosca.

Mrs. Stewart Clark.

Margaret Dickson.

Ulrich Brunner.

W. A. Richardson (when grown in the open).

These roses will make fairly large bushes if after the dead and very weakly shoots have been cut out the remaining ones are lightly pruned ; the ends of the branches should be cut off if they are soft or have been damaged by frost. On the other hand, if it is desired to keep them as reasonably dwarf bushes, two feet high or so, it can be done by pruning them in the orthodox way, that is to say, by shortening the strongest to within five or six buds and pruning weaker ones more severely.

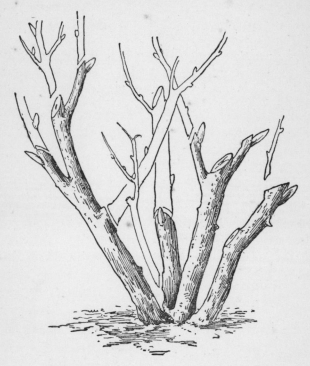

Keep the centre of the bush clear of shoots

Irish Elegance is perhaps an exception, for it will reach a height of six feet if lightly pruned, and indeed makes a good covering for a pillar if planted in well prepared soil :—

A. Hill Gray.

Aspirant Marcel Rouyer.

Betty Uprichard.

C. E. Shea.

Clarice Goodacre.

Caroline Testout.

Dean Hole.

Dorothy Page Roberts.

Duchess of Wellington.

Irish Elegance.

Irish Fireflame.

Isobel.

Joanna Bridge.

K. of K.

Harry Kirk.

Lord Charlemont.

Madame Leon Pain.

Melanie Soupert.

Mrs. Herbert Stevens

Mrs. J. Laing.

Pharisaer

Prince de Bulgarie.

Red Letter Day.

In this group the roses are of free growth, though they do not make such strong shoots as those in the previous class. They remain bushes about two feet high and respond admirably to the orthodox pruning—shortening the strong shoots to from four to six buds and the weakest from one or two to three or four buds :—

Emma Wright.

Etoile de Hollande.

Florence Izzard.

G. C. Waud.

Golden Emblem.

Gorgeous.

Gustav Grunerwald.

General McArthur.

Frances Gaunt.

Hadley.

La France.

Lady Alice Stanley.

Lieutenant Chauré.

Los Angeles.

Madame Abel Chatenay.

Mabel Morse.

Madame Ravary.

Madame E. Herriot.

Margaret Dickson Hamill.

Mrs. Henry Morse.

Hawlmark Crimson.   Mrs. Henry Bowles.
Henrietta.   Mrs. Wemyss Quin.
Hoosier Beauty.   Miss Van Rossem.
Hortulanus Budde.   Mrs. Alfred Tate.
Independence Day.   Ophelia.
Lamia.   Madame Butterfly.
Lady Hillingdon.   Souvenir de Georges
Lady Pirrie.   Pernet.

Although the growth of these roses varies according to the kind of soil and the locality in which they are planted, generally they may be classed as less vigorous than those already named. The usual way of pruning them is carefully to cut out dead and very weakly shoots and to shorten the remainder to from two to four or five buds according to the vigour. Good cultivation and well prepared ground are necessary. It is contended that even some of the weak-growing roses will, if very lightly pruned, make better progress than if pruned in the usual way; if any of the varieties are not satisfactory under the treatment recommended the reader is advised to let them grow as they will, merely taking the precaution to cut out all dead shoots and those that are so weak as obviously to be useless.

Angele Pernet.   Marquise de Sinety.
Captain Kilbee Stuart.   Melody.
Château de Clos Vougeot.   Mrs. Bertram Walker.
Christine.   Mrs. David McKee
Colonel O. Fitzgerald.   Mrs. E. Hicks.

Weeping standard Roses alongside a garden path

Countess Clanwilliam.	Mrs. E. Powell.
Donald McDonald.	Mrs. George Norwood.
Lady Inchiquin.	Mrs. W. J. Grant.
Lady Roberts.	Princess Mary.
Liberty.	Richmond.
Madame Antoine Mari.	Ruth.
Madame Hoste.	Sovereign.
Madame Segond Weber.	Souvenir de Claudius
Molly Sharman Crawford.	Pernet.

This classification of varieties of roses according to the pruning they need must be regarded as a general guide only. Roses vary so much in different gardens that it is impossible to lay down hard-and-fast rules and to advise that they be followed slavishly. For instance, in one garden a variety may grow much more vigorously than in another, and it must be treated accordingly. If, however, the amateur regards this guide as correct until by his own experience of the growth of the roses in his garden he finds it necessary to prune differently, he will at least be able to make a satisfactory beginning and afterwards his own experience will teach a good deal.

Then there are the very vigorous roses which develop naturally into large bushes. These do not need systematic pruning, since it is impossible to keep them dwarf except at the risk of having them full of flowerless shoots. If they are pruned severely in spring in the way that the ordinary bush or dwarf roses are pruned they will

c

merely continue to make vigorous growth and the blossoming will be sparse.

In the spring following planting it is wise to cut out weak shoots and to shorten the remainder to within twelve to fifteen inches of the base. The result of this treatment will be that few blooms will be obtained the first summer, but the plants will make strong growths for the following year's blossoming. In subsequent years the correct practice is, in autumn, to cut out a few of the oldest branches or parts of them and allow the new ones to replace them. In spring it will be necessary to look over the bushes for the purpose of cutting out thin, weakly shoots and shortening the side shoots on the old branches.

The following roses thrive under this system of pruning :—

Conrad Meyer.	Pax.
Danaë.	Penzance Briars.
Grüss an Teplitz.	Prosperity.
Moonlight.	Rugosa (Japanese Briar).
Moyesii.	Sweetbriar.

CHAPTER V

Prune these Roses Lightly

IF, as has been said, the nerve system of a plant is more sensitive than that of a human being, how our poor rose trees must suffer when, armed with secateurs or pruning knife, in the spring of each year we proceed to cut them down to within a few inches of the ground. I am still a believer in hard pruning all newly planted roses, as their root system has not become established, and by pruning any premature strain on the roots is prevented, root and branch growth making progress together. Pruning also encourages strong basal growths as early as possible and thus helps to build up a vigorous, healthy plant.

In succeeding years the question of pruning has to be viewed from a different standpoint. The root system has by then become established, and to prune hard means giving a severe check to the roots. It also discourages the formation of new roots which are vital to the development of top growth. With this theory in mind, for the last few years I have pruned some varieties very lightly, and the results have proved that not only is the vigour of the plant increased but far more blooms of better shape have been produced, and in many cases they have been up to exhibition form. I was led to try the experiment by seeing some bushes of the rose Lady Hillingdon that had been

left practically unpruned for a few years. They were full
of vigour and bearing many fine blooms on long, purple-
coloured stems so characteristic of the variety.

My first tests were made with the roses Clarice Goodacre
and W. C. Clarke, both vigorous varieties. The results
exceeded my expectations. In two years' time the former
had grown into a bush five feet in height, full of strong
growths bearing bunches of bloom which I thinned out.
The outcome was that I had dozens of fine shapely blooms
which made me more than ever pleased with this somewhat neglected rose. The result was similar with W. C.
Clarke, but as this is of somewhat spreading rather than
upright habit of growth the plant was not so tall, but it
developed into a bush of good size.

Pruning Single Roses

The single roses such as Irish Fireflame, Irish Elegance,
Irish Afterglow, etc., I have also treated similarly, with
equally good results. One great advantage of pruning
these single roses lightly is that they come into bloom
much earlier and at a time of the year when the tempera-
ture is lower; thus they last longer in beauty. This type
of rose is very disappointing in hot weather, when the
blooms open so quickly and fade rapidly. If they are
induced to bloom in June they remain in the bud stage
(in which they are lovely) for quite a long time and are
then fine for cutting and buttonholes. Lulu is another
variety that is excellent when lightly pruned.

Many growers will ask, "But do you not do away with

the formation of strong basal growths which are essential to the rejuvenation of the plant?" I feared the same thing, but found that the root action was so strong that

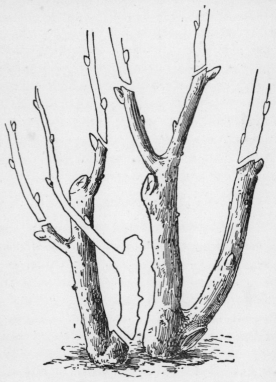

A bush Rose after moderate pruning

good shoots were thrown up from the base, thus allowing the oldest growths to be cut away the next year, thereby thinning out and maintaining the symmetry and vigour of the trees.

I am convinced that the Pernetiana race of roses resents too free use of the knife. Unfortunately these roses have a habit of making thick, pithy growths late in the season; they fail to "ripen" properly, with the result that many of them die back in the winter. In this case there is no alternative but to cut back to sound wood where the pith has not been turned brown. Otherwise the less these roses are pruned the better. The vigorous growth made by Golden Emblem, Mrs. Wemyss Quin, The Queen Alexandra Rose, Ruth, and others of this class, when lightly pruned is astonishing. I have instanced the case of rose Lady Hillingdon, which is a Tea, and I am sure we prune this class of rose too severely as a rule.

Pruning Weakly Rose Trees

We have always been told to prune weakly rose trees much harder than vigorous ones. This again is all right in theory, but I have tried the effect of leaving apparently poor ones almost untouched with the knife to see if a fair amount of branch growth could not be obtained, which would re-act favourably on the root system and so build up a better plant. I was led to do this by my experience with the rose called America, which had made poor growth out of doors until I pruned it lightly, with the result that several promising shoots grew from near the base.

To sum up—if we have limited space, and wish to grow as many roses as possible, we must prune as usual, otherwise our rose beds will become a tangle of growths.

If, on the contrary, we can give them ample space let us try to build up some real rose bushes that will be a sight worth seeing when in full bloom, and by the judicious thinning out of the buds we can obtain a fair percentage of large blooms quite fit for exhibition. A big, shapely rose bush that blossoms freely is a glorious sight, and the amateur will reap a rich reward if he experiments instead of following the copybooks slavishly.

CHAPTER VI

Pegging down Vigorous Rose Trees

SOME rose trees, although commonly classed as bush roses, are so vigorous that obviously it is an incorrect practice to prune them severely. When the beginner has pruned them in the orthodox way for one or two years and has been rewarded by still more vigorous branches and very few blooms, he will begin to wonder whether his practice is the correct one and must come to the conclusion that he has done the wrong thing; and he will be right in that assumption.

In dealing with rose bushes that produce branches 5 or 6 feet long in one season it is a great mistake to prune them hard. That is simply to cut away the shoots that would have yielded a harvest of flowers, while it does nothing to check the development of the strong branches; as a matter of fact the more severely they are pruned the more vigorously do they grow.

What, then, is to be done? The proper way to deal with these varieties is in spring to adopt the practice known as "pegging down." Thin weakly shoots are first cut out and the tips of the others are cut off if they are thin or soft. No further pruning is done unless of course any of the branches are dead or decaying; they ought to be cut right out then, for they do harm to the tree.

The actual work of pegging down is simple enough, for it consists merely in fastening the end of the branch in the ground. The result is to bend the branch in, roughly, the shape of a semi-circle or low arch. The best way of securing the end of the branch in the ground is by means of a stout wooden peg. The precaution ought also to be taken of tying the end of the branch securely to the peg and to knock the latter firmly in the soil, for if it were suddenly to spring up when the grower was tending his plants it might cause an injury.

Effect of Pegging Down

During the summer all such pegged-down branches will start into growth at almost every bud throughout their full length and most of the shoots will produce flowers, with the result that a first-rate display is obtained. It must have been noticed by all who grow rose trees that if a branch is left upright it will start to grow only at the top, remaining bare of shoots at the base. By pegging down the branch in the way described the lower buds are forced into growth and the result is seen in shoots and flowers all along it.

Pruning after Flowering

What shall be done with the pegged-down branch after the flowers are over? Normally the rose tree will produce other vigorous branches to take the place of the old ones which have blossomed, and the latter can therefore be cut right out when they are no longer of any value, in other words when they have ceased to bear flowers. Sometimes, however, a new and vigorous shoot will start to grow on the pegged-down branch at some distance from the base and only the part of the old branch above that point can be cut away.

Above all things it is necessary to take care of fresh, strong shoots for another year. If by some mischance

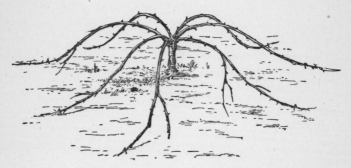

Branches of Rose tree pegged down

these are not forthcoming, then the old pegged-down branches must be allowed to remain and in the following spring the side shoots, those that produced blooms the previous year, are shortened to within two or three buds of the base. Such blooms will not be so fine as those obtained directly from the branch, but they will be numerous. It is, however, rarely that some new branches do not develop.

It is clear that rose bushes treated in this manner take up a good deal more room than those pruned in the orthodox way, and if the space cannot be spared for them

In pruning
Dwarfs retain the
best branches and
shorten to within 3 or 4
buds of where
growth started
last season.

Newly planted Bush Roses
require hard pruning

Some vigorously
growing Roses
should not be
hard pruned
it is best to peg down the
long shoots, these will produce plenty of blooms

then the alternative is to grow varieties that respond to more severe pruning.

Among the roses that grow so vigorously that they cannot be pruned severely every year without being spoilt, yet thrive splendidly when their branches are pegged down, are Hugh Dickson, George Dickson, Frau Karl Druschki, William Allen Richardson, Lady Waterlow, Gruss an Teplitz, La Tosca, Avoca, H. E. Richardson, J. B. Clark, Mrs. Stewart Clark, Zephirin Drouhin (the Thornless Rose), Sarah Bernhardt, Gloire de Dijon, Clio, and others mentioned in Chapter V.

As these long shoots or branches are liable to be blown about and damaged, and to loosen the hold of the tree itself in the ground, it is essential to make them secure before stormy weather sets in in autumn. They should be tied to temporary supports.

CHAPTER VII

Pruning Newly Planted Rose Trees

WHETHER severe pruning annually throughout the life of a rose tree is beneficial or not—and there is a good deal to be said for both points of view—there can be little or no doubt that it is wise to prune newly planted rose trees severely. It has often been said that the rose tree you buy from the nurseryman is valuable or otherwise according to the condition of its roots. If these are fibrous and numerous then the rose tree may be expected to thrive; if, however, they are thick and fibreless and few in number the tree's chances are not so good, or at least it will take longer to become established.

The branches on bought rose trees are not regarded as of permanent value, for the usual practice is to cut them back hard, leaving only two or three buds on each, and from these an entirely new rose bush is built up in due course. This seems very drastic treatment, but it pays; if the plant is healthy the few remaining buds will give rise to strong shoots that form the foundation of a satisfactory bush. In later years pruning may be severe, moderate, or light, according to the objects of the grower and the variety dealt with, but the first pruning should be severe, thus almost the whole of the top growth of the rose bush will be renewed.

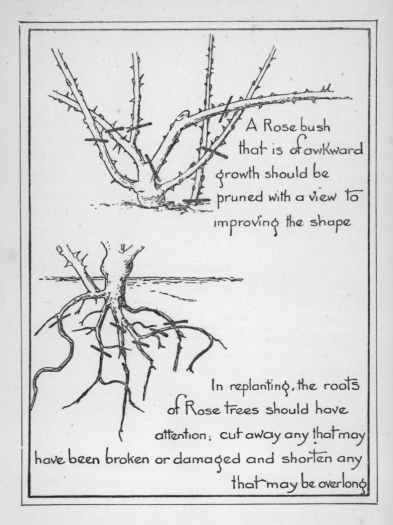

A Rose bush
that is of awkward
growth should be
pruned with a view to
improving the shape

In replanting, the roots
of Rose trees should have
attention; cut away any that may
have been broken or damaged and shorten any
that may be overlong

This severe cutting back has the effect of forcing the lowest buds to break into growth and ensures the correct beginning of a shapely bush, whereas if the shoots are left long, growth will be toward the top only, and the chances are that the lower part will remain bare.

Most rose trees are planted in autumn, and the first pruning is in March or April of the following year. Many trees, however, are planted in spring, and it is imperative that these be pruned severely if they are to have a chance of making good growth the first summer. But the beginner will be well advised to prune all his newly planted rose trees hard and not be tempted to leave the branches six or eight inches long, as many inexperienced amateurs do.

Pruning Newly Planted Rambler Roses

Even rambler roses ought to be pruned hard in the spring following planting. All the stems should be cut down to within six inches or so of the ground. If that is done the tree will send up several lusty young shoots in early summer that will be six feet or more high and will have reached the top of the support by the end of the season. If it is wished to leave a few of the old stems in order to have a few blooms the first summer, it may be done with possibly little disadvantage; most of the ramblers are so vigorous that they are likely to make satisfactory growth whichever method is adopted. But the safest plan is to cut down all the stems, for the poor flower display that will result from the other method is scarcely sufficient reward for the slight risk of indifferent growth that is run in leaving the old stems unpruned.

What one has to make sure of is vigorous growth that will blossom the following summer, and that will certainly result if the stems are cut down; the new shoots may be neither so numerous nor so strong if the old stems are left for the sake of the few blooms they will produce. Even if the old stems are left the flower display is certain to be an indifferent one, and it is far better to sacrifice these than to run the risk of interfering with the vigorous growth of the rose tree and thus jeopardise next year's blossoming.

These Roses Need Special Care

The pruning of newly planted rose trees of the various climbing "sports," e.g. Climbing Ophelia, Climbing Mrs. Grant, Climbing Richmond, and so on, needs special care. As is explained on page 57, these roses are accidental variations or "sports" from the dwarf or bush roses of the same name and if they are pruned incorrectly it is possible that they will revert to the dwarf or non-climbing type.

When newly planted, these roses must not be pruned severely, otherwise they may never climb at all. The branches ought to be left almost untouched. If the ends are soft, thin, or shrivelled they must of course be cut off, and if the tree possesses four or five stems one of them may be shortened to within 6 or 8 inches of the ground, but no further pruning is necessary or advisable. Later in

An ideal Rose garden. Arches of climbing and rambling Roses surround the formal beds on the lawn

Plant bush Roses about 18" apart.

Prune newly planted Ramblers to within 6 inches of the ground.

Prune newly planted bush Roses to 2 buds from base of last Summer's shoots.

D

the year or the following spring it will be possible to cut out one or more of the old stems if fresh, vigorous shoots have developed meanwhile. But it is of no avail to attempt to force these climbing "sports" to produce fresh stems by pruning the existing ones severely; that method is likely to prove very disappointing, though occasionally it may succeed. The risk, however, is too great, and readers are advised to wait until the tree has made good growth before the old stems are cut out. In subsequent years the method of pruning is to cut away old stems or parts of them to the extent that they can be replaced by other and younger ones.

CHAPTER VIII

Pruning Standard Rose Trees

IF the pruning of bush or dwarf rose trees is understood there will be little difficulty in dealing with standard rose trees, for these are the same varieties budded on top of a tall stem instead of near the ground. Thus if the amateur knows how to prune rose Madame Abel Chatenay, for instance, when this variety is grown as a dwarf or bush, he will be able to prune it equally well in standard form.

Newly planted standard rose trees ought to be pruned severely, just as was advised for the dwarfs, but in subsequent years fairly light pruning seems to suit most of them best. In planting a collection of standard roses it is necessary to choose varieties that are suitable for the purpose, for some make better "heads" than others. The free-growing varieties give greatest satisfaction; these, if pruned lightly, make good heads of branches in the course of time and are then very handsome.

Although it has nothing to do with the actual work of pruning, a hint that was published in *Popular Gardening* from a reader some time ago is worth mentioning because it appears to show why some, and probably many, newly planted standard rose trees fail. Owing to the root disturbance occasioned by transplanting the sap does

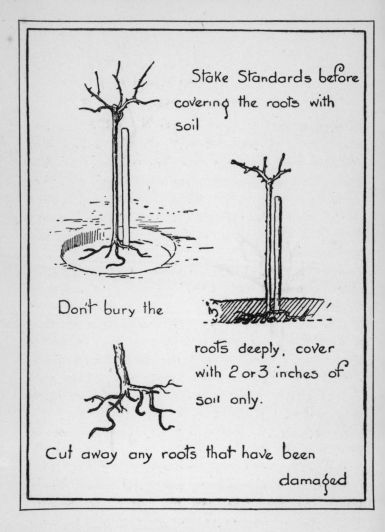

Stake Standards before covering the roots with soil

Don't bury the

roots deeply, cover with 2 or 3 inches of soil only.

Cut away any roots that have been damaged

Standard Roses
usually need drastic
thinning and pruning
at the end of March

Remove weakly &
superfluous growths
and any dead wood, cut back
strong shoots less than weak
ones

A clean cut
from below a bud and
upwards is necessary
for good pruning

not flow freely up the long stem of the tree, and as a consequence the head of branches is starved for the time being, and by the time the roots are growing freely the branches may have become so weakened as to be beyond recovery. The plan adopted by this correspondent was to wrap cloth round the stem after planting the trees and to keep it always moist by syringeing when necessary. This had a remarkable effect on the trees, and was the means not only of saving some of them from total failure, but it helped them to grow freely and to make good "heads."

Pruning New Standards

Thinning out weak and dead shoots from the standard roses is a detail of importance and is the first thing to be done in pruning ; the remaining branches are then shortened and the problem to solve is how far they should be cut back. In the spring following planting they ought to be cut to within two or three buds of the base of the previous summer's growth, not any lower, as I have seen done. In subsequent years it is usually sufficient to shorten the past summer's shoots by about half, or even less than that when dealing with such as Hugh Dickson, Frau Karl Druschki, Caroline Testout, La Tosca, and other free growing varieties. It is important always to cut to a bud that points outward so that a well balanced head of branches may result and there will then be no risk of the centre being filled up.

The pruning of weeping standards, which consist of

To obtain good blooms most Roses need hard pruning. For Standards" cut away all weak growths & shorten the others.

Some kinds are inclined to throw up one shoot much more vigorous than the rest, this should be pruned hard or the others may die

Always cut back to an outside bud to avoid a crowded centre

rambler and climbing roses budded on the top of tall stems, is carried out much in the same way as when those roses are grown naturally. That is to say, at the end of the summer or early in autumn such old branches or parts of them as can be replaced by young shoots of the past summer's growth are cut out, the latter taking their places. As a rule fresh shoots are not produced so freely as when the rambler and climbing roses are grown naturally on arches and pillars, and care must be taken not to cut out more old wood than can be replaced by young shoots. Though the latter will yield the finest display of bloom the following year, the side shoots on the old branches will also flower if they are cut back in spring to two or three buds.

CHAPTER IX

Pruning Rambler Roses

THESE are the easiest of all rose trees to prune. It is but necessary to realise that the best display of blossom is provided by the shoots or stems which grew during the previous summer in order to understand exactly how the pruning should be carried out. The only difficulty likely to confront the beginner will arise in dealing with different varieties, because they vary a good deal in their habit of growth, therefore they cannot all be pruned by rule of thumb; each one must be dealt with as it needs.

Let us take a well-known and typical rambler rose, Dorothy Perkins, Hiawatha, or American Pillar. So far as their pruning is concerned any one of these may be taken as an example for their manner of growth is similar though they vary in vigour. They produce fresh shoots or stems from somewhere near the base, often at the ground level, every summer, and it is these that will yield the chief flower display the following year. Thus the pruning consists in cutting out the old stems when the blooms are over; the fresh shoots are then tied to the support to replace them. The work of pruning is carried out at the end of summer or early in autumn, for the ramblers are summer flowering only, though some

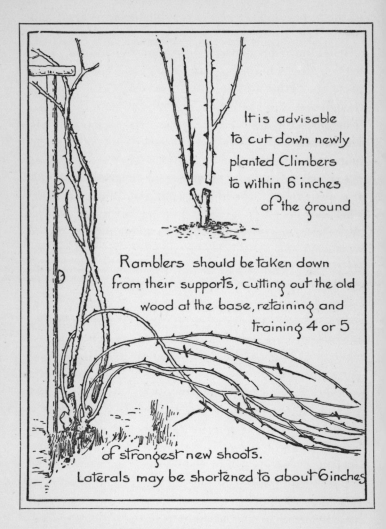

It is advisable to cut down newly planted Climbers to within 6 inches of the ground

Ramblers should be taken down from their supports, cutting out the old wood at the base, retaining and training 4 or 5 of strongest new shoots.

Laterals may be shortened to about 6 inches

of them may and do bear a few blooms in August and September.

If the new shoots are few in number—and that may happen after a hot, dry summer—it would be a mistake to cut out all the old stems, for these will produce flowers, though they will not be so numerous or so fine as those from one-year-old stems. If any old stems are left the side shoots on them must be shortened to three or four buds in spring.

Let us take another rambler rose of a different type of growth from those already named—Alberic Barbier. The branches of this variety become thick and woody at the base and as a rule the fresh shoots arise on them at some distance from the ground. Thus the pruning needed is very similar to that advised when dealing with the climbing roses, except that parts of old branches can usually be removed much more freely because there are more new shoots to replace them. The branches must be cut back only to where the new shoots arise.

In spring there will be more pruning to be done than when dealing with varieties of the Dorothy Perkins type, because of the greater number of side shoots on those parts of the old branches that were perforce allowed to remain; these side shoots are shortened to within three or four buds of the main branches from which they sprang.

The most convenient way of pruning rambler rose trees of the Hiawatha, Dorothy Perkins, and American Pillar type is to detach all the stems from their supports, lay them on the ground, cut out the old ones that can be spared, and then tie the fresh ones in position. This, however, cannot very well be done with ramblers that become woody at the base like Alberic Barbier.

When rambler roses are grown as pillars and are trained on tall poles it is a good plan to shorten some of the stems in spring, thus ensuring flowers almost from top to base; if all the stems are left of equal length the display of blossom will be chiefly at the top of the pillar.

It should be mentioned that the rambler rose Emily Gray should be left unpruned for the first two or three years as it is "shy flowering." Subsequently the older branches may be cut out as they can be spared.

CHAPTER X

Pruning Climbing Roses

IN considering the pruning of climbing roses as distinct from rambler roses, which are dealt with in another chapter, it is convenient to separate them into two groups; typical examples are Madame Alfred Carrière and Paul's Scarlet Climber in one group, and Climbing Caroline Testout and Climbing Richmond in the other.

The first group consists of vigorous climbing roses belonging chiefly to the hybrid tea class, though a few of the varieties concerned are included in other classes. Typical examples in addition to those two named above are Gloire de Dijon, William Allen Richardson, Bouquet d'Or, François Crousse, and others of similar growth. In the cultivation of these roses, whether they are planted against an arch or a wall, one is faced with the fact that they are liable to become bare of shoots and leaves at the base, with the result that in a few years they are rather unsightly. Correct pruning can do something to remedy this trouble, but as a rule it does not do away with it altogether. However, in the attempt to prevent the trees getting bare at the base we shall be in a fair way towards pruning them properly.

The chief thing to remember is that these roses bear the best flowers and the greatest number of them on the branches of the previous summer's growth; the greater number of these the trees possess the finer will be the display of bloom. In pruning, therefore, we must cut out as many as possible of the branches that are more than one year old—just as many, in fact, as can be replaced by younger ones.

When to Prune Climbing Roses

The best time to prune climbing rose trees is in early autumn, when the last of the flowers has faded. As some varieties bloom more or less continuously it would be unwise to prune earlier in the season as we should run the risk of cutting away shoots that might bear late summer or early autumn blooms. The extent to which those old branches which have bloomed can be cut out must be governed by the number of new ones of the current summer's growth that are available for tying in to replace them. The nearer the base of the tree the latter have developed the better, for the old branches can be cut right down to where the new ones started.

Bending Down the Branches

It happens frequently that the new shoot begins to grow part of the way up the old branch and not from the base of the tree, and the old wood can be cut out only at a point just above it. It is for this reason that the lowest branches are apt to get bare. This fault can sometimes be remedied by bending down (as low as it can be brought down without breaking) one of the

If using secateurs for pruning
see that the nut is well adjusted and
that they make a clean cut.

Climbers need little
spring pruning,
tops nipped

by frost should be cut back and
old wood removed.

Pruning the leaders of climbers
to various heights from the ground
is a good plan.

branches, in the hope that it will be forced to start into growth at the base. Even if the method recommended does not altogether prevent the lower part getting rather bare it will at all events prevent the tree from becoming unsightly and will keep it full of fresh branches that will yield the maximum number of blooms.

If new shoots are produced in insufficient numbers to allow of old branches being cut out freely, the only thing to do is to retain some of the latter, and in spring to prune their side shoots back to two or three buds. They will yield flowers, but these will not be so fine as those from the one-year-old branches.

Training Climbing Rose Trees

The way in which climbing rose trees are trained makes all the difference to their well-being. If the branches are allowed to grow upright and are more or less bunched together, shoots and flowers will appear only towards the top; if the lowest branches are trained as nearly horizontally as possible and the remainder in gradually rising tiers so that eventually the tree is roughly fan-shaped, there will be less risk of bareness at the base, and the flowers will be more numerous and distributed more evenly.

When climbing roses are grown for the purpose of covering a pillar or tall pole it is obvious that they cannot be spread out, but must be tied in perpendicularly; in such a case it is a good plan to leave some of the branches full length, to shorten others by one third, and one or two by as much as a half, for the purpose of having the pillar covered with leaves and flowers almost from top to bottom.

Pruning Climbing "Sports"

The second group of climbing roses to which reference was made in the opening paragraph of this chapter consists of climbing "sports" of various popular dwarf or bush roses. It may be as well first of all to explain what a sport is : it is an accidental variation from the original variety and may take the form of a change in the colour of the flowers or a change in the habit of growth; a variety that has hitherto been of dwarf growth may suddenly and for no accountable reason develop into a climber. If buds are taken from this and budded on a suitable stock the climbing habit of growth is perpetuated and we have a climbing variety of a rose that formerly was known only to exist as a low bush. In this way such varieties as Climbing Richmond, Climbing Ophelia, Climbing Lady Hillingdon, and many more have been obtained.

The Meaning of "Sports"

They are known as "sports" because they originated from an accidental change of growth in the bush variety of the same name; this began to climb and the climbing form was made permanent by budding. These roses still retain the original name prefixed by the word "climbing," because they are identical in flower; the

E

only difference between them and the dwarf varieties from which they sprang is that they grow tall and the others remain dwarf.

The advice already given in respect of pruning other climbing rose trees applies also to the climbing "sports." They are perhaps rather more difficult to manage because they do not produce fresh shoots or branches so freely, but if the recommendations given earlier in this chapter are observed it ought not to be difficult to maintain them in a healthy condition. The chief point to bear in mind is in autumn to cut out all the old branches or parts of them that can be replaced by those of the past summer's growth.

In spring there is little further pruning to be done; its extent must depend on the way in which the trees have passed through the winter. If the tips of the branches are soft and withered they must of course be cut off. If one or two old branches were left because there were not enough new ones to take their places it will be necessary to prune the side shoots on these to three buds.

One important matter concerning the pruning of the climbing "sports" must be remembered. As is mentioned in another chapter, it is the usual practice to prune newly planted rose trees severely, but climbing "sports" must not be treated in this way or they may refuse to climb. The details of pruning newly planted rose trees are given in a chapter dealing with this subject.

CHAPTER XI

Pruning Various Other Roses

A FEW words may be said concerning the pruning of other types of roses that are popular at the present time. The musk-scented shrub roses are now widely grown; in the course of a few years they develop into large bushes and flower during summer and autumn. They need little pruning—in autumn they ought to be looked over for the purpose of cutting out a few of the oldest branches, or parts of them, to give more space for those of the past summer's growth. In spring it will probably be necessary to shorten the side shoots on the old branches, but no severe cutting back must be done.

The dwarf polyantha or baby rambler roses have been greatly improved during recent years, and there are now some excellent and showy varieties. If it is wished to keep them as low bushes the shoots may be pruned back to from four to six buds in spring after dead and useless pieces have been cut out. If, however, large bushes are wanted, the shoots should be shortened only slightly, but all very weak ones must be cut right out.

China roses, pernetiana roses, and tea roses often need very little pruning, because their shoots suffer during the winter. When the dead and very weak parts have been cut away there is little left to be done except slightly to shorten those remaining. These classes of roses usually thrive best when the sound shoots are pruned lightly.

Moss roses are not widely cultivated nowadays, possibly because there are so many other varieties that make a much more satisfactory show in the garden. The best way to deal with them is to plant them in well-prepared and enriched ground, to restrict the number of shoots by cutting out all weakly and small ones, and to shorten them by about one-half in spring.

The yellow banksian rose (which is more satisfactory than the white one) is sometimes used for planting against a sunny house-wall, and complaints of its non-flowering are frequent. The reason is generally found in incorrect pruning. Few flowers are likely to be produced for several years, but when the tree is well established and of considerable size it ought to bloom well if pruned properly. The small twiggy shoots are those that are most likely to blossom, and they ought not to be cut away. If pruning is found necessary to keep the tree within bounds, or to prevent overcrowding, some of the young vigorous shoots should be removed.

PART II
PRUNING FRUIT TREES
CHAPTER XII
A General Survey

WHEN he has embarked on the cultivation of fruit trees the amateur will find that some knowledge of pruning is essential to enable him to obtain satisfactory results. The rule-of-thumb methods are easily acquired, and an understanding of them is essential as a foundation, though the grower will discover that he must consider not only the characteristics of different varieties, but those of the individual tree if he is to get the very best results from his orchard or fruit garden.

It is true to say that on the whole fruit trees are pruned too severely and that they would bear heavier crops if they were pruned less. A common fault is to plant too large a number of fruit trees in a limited area. In a few years they take up more room than the planter thought they would do, and he finds that annually they become more crowded. Having bought the trees and tended them for a number of years he is somewhat naturally disinclined to do away with any of them, and the only other way of making room for them is to cut back the branches hard. The result is a luxuriant growth of leaves and branches, but the harvest of fruit is a sparse one.

Fruit trees must have room for their proper development; the branches must be fully exposed to air and light, otherwise a successful issue cannot be expected. Then the kind of soil and the position in which they are planted are important matters intimately bound up with the question of pruning.

Why Fruit Trees Fail

If planted in rich soil young fruit trees will grow very vigorously, but they will not bear fruit, at any rate for a number of years, and the more the branches are pruned the more freely do they grow. In the end the owner probably gives up fruit cultivation as a bad job owing to the disappointment year after year of scanty crops.

Although fruit trees need deeply cultivated soil, this ought not to be heavily manured; old mortar rubble or lime rubble is excellent material to mix with the soil for all fruit trees, and especially for the stone fruits, e.g. cherry and plum.

A Matter of Importance

Another point of importance is, when planting, to keep the uppermost roots within three or four inches of the surface of the soil. Deep planting is not conducive to fertility.

It will thus be seen that the necessity for severe pruning, which rarely pays in fruit cultivation, can be prevented by attention to other details—the preparation of the ground, planting and giving the trees sufficient room for their development. The first instruction, therefore, in pruning trees is a negative one—prune them as little as possible consistent with keeping them within the allotted space and preventing overcrowding of the shoots and branches. More abundant crops will be the reward.

CHAPTER XIII

Pruning Newly Planted Fruit Trees

WHAT is a newly planted fruit tree? It is one that has been put in the ground some time between October and March, and of which the pruning is attended to in the spring months following the planting. Thus it may have been in the ground for six months or only for one month.

In dealing with the pruning of such trees two methods are in general practice, and the amateur must decide which one he will follow. The advice of one school is to prune the trees in the first spring; the advice of the opposing school is not to prune until a year later. The latter recommendation, however, now finds less support than formerly, and the beginner may be advised to disregard it and to prune his trees during the spring months (March or early April) that follow the planting.

It is a safe rule to prune newly planted fruit trees severely; unless the branches are cut back fairly hard they are unlikely to start into growth except at the top, and the lower parts may remain bare for all time, thus giving rise to an ill-balanced and unshapely tree. By how much shall they be shortened? and which are the branches to be cut? Those are two pertinent questions. Let us answer the last one first.

It is important that the amateur should realise that

A pruning outfit. Secateurs are included by amateurs generally. Cutting tools must be kept sharp

Stockholm Tar and Lead Paint used for painting the exposed surface after sawing off a limb.

Pare off all rough edges neatly before applying tar or paint

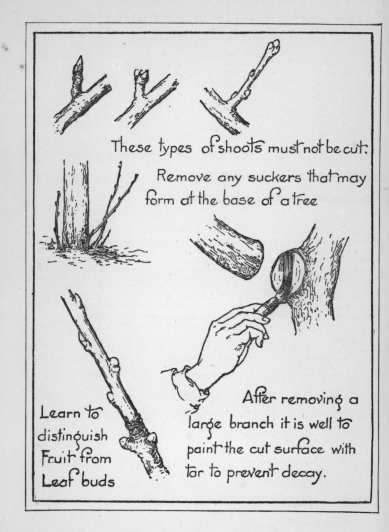

These types of shoots must not be cut.

Remove any suckers that may form at the base of a tree

Learn to distinguish Fruit from Leaf buds

After removing a large branch it is well to paint the cut surface with tar to prevent decay.

in pruning fruit trees the only branches he must cut are those that grew during the past summer; he must not, except in special circumstances, interfere with those that are older. They should be shortened by from one-half to one-third; in other words, they should be left half as long or two-thirds as long as they were.

If the branches are somewhat weakly it will pay to cut them back to such an extent that only one-third is left; if they are moderately vigorous let them be shortened by one-half; if they are really strong and thick, and the trees were planted in autumn, they may need to be shortened by only one-third. It is, however, safer to prune severely. If the trees have been in the ground only a month or two the branches ought not to be left more than half as long as they were. Trees planted late in spring are slow in starting into growth, and their progress the first season may be poor; it certainly will be if they are pruned lightly, but if pruned severely the chances are that the buds towards the base will be forced into growth and will produce good branches.

During the first few years the object ought to be to build up a shapely tree furnished with the requisite number of branches; if the foundation is well and truly laid fruit production will follow as a matter of course. If, however, the tree is pruned lightly the first year, the branches being left at almost full length for the sake of the few fruits they may bear, the chances of the tree having a satisfactory life are jeopardised. Thin, weakly branches cannot bear a heavy crop of fruit.

Therefore at this first pruning do not trouble to consider the question of a crop. Prune hard for the purpose of securing good strong branches that will provide a firm foundation on which the tree can be built up. In later years the pruning can be modified according to the needs of the grower, the kind of tree, and the variety of fruit.

Thin, weakly shoots should be cut right out for they will block up the centre of the tree and crowd the main branches. If there are side shoots on the lower parts of the branches which have been shortened they should be pruned to within two buds of the latter.

The theory of those who advocate deferring the pruning of newly planted fruit trees until March or April twelve months or more after planting is that by that time they will have become established and will respond better to severe pruning. This method may be advisable if fruit trees are grown on poor land where growth is slow unless care is taken to keep the roots moist in dry weather, but generally it is better to prune in the March or April immediately following planting.

CHAPTER XIV

Pruning Standard Fruit Trees

APPLE, pear, plum, cherry, and damson are the fruits commonly grown as standards. Though when dealing with established trees the ways of pruning differ to some extent, standards may conveniently be considered together for the general treatment is similar. The initial pruning of newly planted standards is important, for it exercises a considerable influence on the form and solidity of the tree. The foundation of the branches must be firmly laid; unless they are strong the tree will scarcely be able to bear the weight of a heavy crop, and disfigured and broken limbs will be the result. Therefore the pruning of the newly planted standard must be severe.

All thin and weakly shoots should be cut right out and the main branches shortened to within about 18 inches of the base of the past summer's growth. Then the buds will start growing strongly and the tree will have a firm foundation of branches. For the first few years it will be necessary carefully to regulate the development of the branches by shortening the leading shoots, those at the ends of the branches, by about half in winter, by cutting out all weak growths and by shortening the side shoots on the main branches in summer, and in winter, in the way already explained in the chapter dealing with the pruning of apple trees.

In later years, when the trees are of a fair size and well established, the chief thing to aim at is to keep the main branches well apart and to cut right out any weakly or otherwise useless shoots; if left they will cause over-crowding, and will effectually put an end to fruitfulness. Thinning out is the most important detail in the pruning of standard fruit trees, not cutting back. If the branches are about 18 inches from each other fruit buds will develop naturally along them in due course, and there will be little cutting back to be done either in summer or in winter.

It will, of course, be necessary to look over the trees both in July and in January for the purpose of shortening the side shoots, but if the above directions are observed this work will not be arduous.

The failure of standard trees is generally due to overcrowding; unless the branches have the full benefit of sunlight and air the fruit buds will not develop, the trees will continue to grow freely, and ultimately they will be crowded with thin, useless shoots that are unable to bear fruits themselves and prevent others doing so.

One is often asked what can be done with standard trees that have reached this state. They are full of weak, spindling shoots that never bear fruits, and they have been so neglected that they have developed into a thicket of growth. The first thing is to cut the inside shoots right out. Then the number of branches must be limited; as has been said, they should be about 18 inches apart. Old and worn-out fruit spurs should be shortened, or cut out if they are crowded, and side shoots that have been allowed to grow unchecked should be cut back to within two or three buds of the main branches on which they developed.

CHAPTER XV

Pruning Cordon Trees

THE fruits most commonly grown in the form of cordons are apple and pear. The plum is occasionally grown in this form, but it is not very satisfactory, and amateurs who wish to grow plums are advised to purchase pyramid or standard trees.

A cordon tree is one that is restricted to one stem, or two or three stems; it has no branches other than the annually shortened side shoots, which eventually become "spurs," on which blossom buds and fruits are borne. It is obvious that trees of this kind must be pruned severely, otherwise they would soon branch out, lose their characteristic shape, and cease to be cordons.

So far as their actual pruning is concerned, there is little to be said beyond that it must proceed on the conventional lines referred to in the chapter dealing with the pruning of apple trees. The leading shoot, that which extends the stem, is allowed to develop naturally in the summer, but in winter it is shortened by one-half or one-third, according to whether it is rather weakly or vigorous. In July or August the side shoots are shortened to within about six buds of the base of the current summer's growth, not counting the small leaves at the bottom, and in winter they are further cut back to within two buds or so.

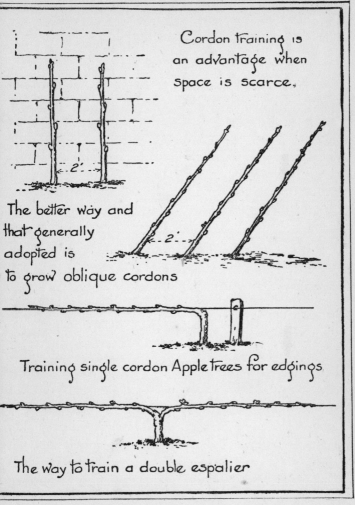

Cordon training is an advantage when space is scarce.

The better way and that generally adopted is to grow oblique cordons

Training single cordon Apple trees for edgings

The way to train a double espalier

F

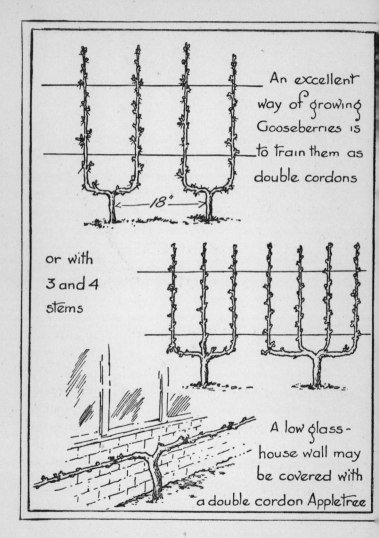

An excellent way of growing Gooseberries is to train them as double cordons

18"

or with 3 and 4 stems

A low glass-house wall may be covered with a double cordon Appletree

This is certainly rule-of-thumb pruning, but it is the only thing to do if the shape of the tree is to be preserved. It does not suit all varieties, of course, and when choosing apple trees to be grown as cordons it is wise to avoid those of vigorous or otherwise unsuitable growth, such as Newton Wonder, Bramley's Seedling, Lane's Prince Albert, and Norfolk Beauty.

In the course of years the original stem may become weakly, with the result that the spurs lose vigour and do not blossom and fruit satisfactorily. This matter can be remedied by training up another stem to take the place of the original one and eventually cutting out the latter altogether. The process is a gradual one, and takes several years to accomplish.

When this course is deemed necessary a promising shoot as low down in the tree as possible should be taken care of and allowed to grow unchecked during the summer months. At the winter pruning it is cut back to within 15 inches of the base. Every year it is allowed to progress to that extent; thus in the course of three years it will be nearly 4 feet high. Then the work of getting rid of the old stem may be begun. This should gradually be shortened as the new stem makes progress, until in the course of time it is cut away altogether and the new stem takes its place. By adopting this method cordon apple trees can be kept in a healthy and fruitful state for an indefinite period.

CHAPTER XVI

Pruning Trained Fruit Trees

TRAINED fruit trees are those grown against a wall or on a special support in the open garden. They are of various shapes, chief of which are the single cordon, double-stemmed, treble-stemmed, and gridiron or four-stemmed cordons, fan-shaped and horizontal. Peach, nectarine, and apricot are commonly grown only as fan-shaped trees; but apple, pear, plum, and cherry are grown in both forms, though the latter is generally trained as a fan-shaped tree.

When the trees are young it is necessary to prune and train them carefully for the purpose of obtaining tiers of branches at a uniform distance from each other on the horizontal espaliers and to preserve the shape of the fan-shaped tree.

Amateurs would do well to obtain trees three or four years old and not to attempt to train them from "maidens." In pruning horizontal espaliers the side shoots must be "stopped" or cut off at about the sixth leaf in summer and shortened again in winter, and the shoots at the ends of the branches—the leading shoots, as they are called—are shortened by about half in winter.

In the following spring care must be taken to select a

Maiden tree headed
to 4 eyes for fan training

The second
stage of fan
training proper

Apple & Pear trees train well as espaliers
    allowing about 15' between the trees
                also along a path.

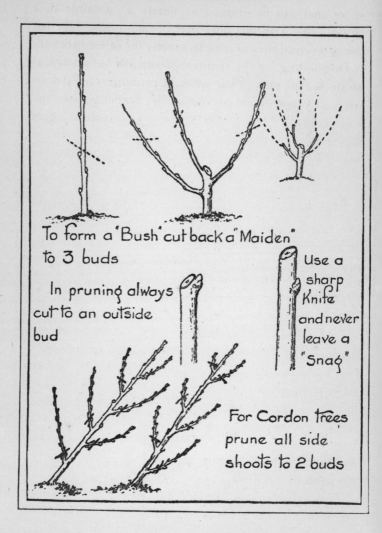

To form a "Bush" cut back a "Maiden" to 3 buds

In pruning always cut to an outside bud

Use a sharp Knife and never leave a "Snag"

For Cordon trees prune all side shoots to 2 buds

shoot that can be trained as nearly as possible in a straight line with the older part of each branch, so that the latter continues to grow in exactly the same direction.

Disbudding, or the removal of superfluous shoots, is an important part of the work of pruning trained fruit trees; it saves much cutting of the branches later on, and unnecessary branch pruning is to be avoided. Side shoots must, however, be pruned in summer and in winter in order to preserve the symmetry of the tree.

Prune Top of Tree First

In summer it is wise to prune the upper part of the tree before the lower part, and to restrict the sub-lateral or secondary shoots to one leaf, because the tendency of the tree is to grow more strongly at the top than at the bottom; by allowing the shoots on the lower branches rather more freedom a more uniform growth will be obtained.

It is difficult to keep fan-shaped trees of peach and nectarine in good condition and shapely unless great care is taken to preserve young shoots as near the base as possible, so that they may be tied in to replace the older branches when, after the fruits have been gathered, these are cut out. In fact, it is not an easy matter to keep trained fruit trees of any kind in a healthy and fruitful condition unless they are given frequent attention and skilled care.

The trees soon become ill-balanced unless the vigorous shoots are restricted and the weaker ones encouraged by allowing them rather more freedom of growth. Above all, it is essential to prevent the top of the tree making vigorous growth to the detriment and weakening of the lower branches. The latter are likely to die, with the result that the form of the tree is spoilt and it is difficulty to restore it when the tree is no longer young.

CHAPTER XVII

Summer Pruning

THE pruning practised during the summer months is of real importance in the cultivation of fruit trees; if it is neglected, satisfactory results are not likely to be obtained. It consists in shortening those shoots that are not required to extend the branches, thus preventing overcrowding and exposing the buds on the lower parts of the shoots—those of chief importance—to sunlight and air, and assisting in their development.

When fruit trees are cultivated in a restricted area pruning is essential to prevent the shoots and branches from becoming crowded, and to direct the development of the trees in the ways desired. If summer pruning is not practised a good deal of the growth that formed during the summer months will have to be cut away in winter since room cannot be found for it. It must surely be to the advantage of the trees that they should be prevented from making these superfluous shoots than that the latter should be allowed to grow and afterwards be cut away. At all events, that is the view taken by the professional gardener, and summer pruning has been an established practice in gardens for generations.

It is a matter of importance to prune at the right time. It cannot be said that one period is suitable for

When pruning use a very sharp Knife.

or if using Secateurs see that they are sharp, the nut well adjusted and that they make a clean cut.

Leading shoots should be left alone at present unless they are crowding out others or are in any way damaged or diseased.

One object of
Summer Pruning is
to secure the admission
of Sunshine and Air
among the branches
when the trees are in leaf

Unripened fruit & buds
cannot flourish if the trees are
overcrowded with
useless growth.

Summer pruned trees
with open centres have a
chance.

all fruit trees. Those grown against sunny walls and
fences are much more advanced in growth by early
July than others in the open garden, obviously
therefore they need attention earlier in the summer
than the latter. Such trees ought to be summer pruned
during the first fortnight in July; the exact time must
depend on the condition of the shoots. When these are
seven or eight inches long they ought to be pruned. It
is usually found best to summer prune fruit trees in the
open garden towards the end of July and early in August.

Pruning the Side Shoots

The pruning consists of shortening (by cutting or
pinching off with finger and thumb) the shoots of the
current summer's growth other than those at the ends
of the branches. It is the usual practice to leave these
unpruned until winter. Most gardeners recommend
leaving six leaves on each of the summer side shoots,
the small leaves at the extreme base not being included.
If the shoots are cut down much lower than this there
is a possibility that the buds at the base will start into
growth, and we do not want that to happen until the
following spring.

Pruning Sub-laterals

A few weeks after the shoots have been pruned or
"stopped" in this way, the buds in the axils of the
uppermost leaves will start to grow, and the shoots they
produce are known as sub-laterals. They are of no per-

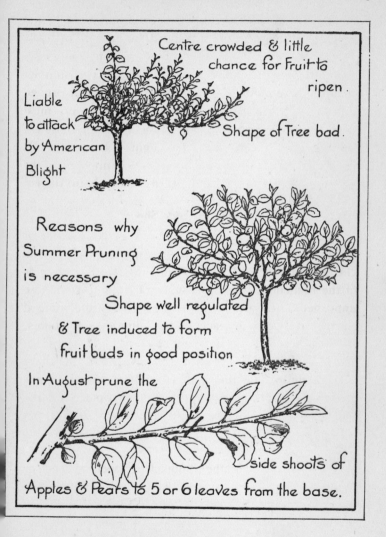

Centre crowded & little chance for Fruit to ripen.

Liable to attack by American Blight

Shape of Tree bad.

Reasons why Summer Pruning is necessary

Shape well regulated & Tree induced to form fruit buds in good position

In August prune the

side shoots of Apples & Pears to 5 or 6 leaves from the base.

Should Sub-lateral shoots form, leave them to be

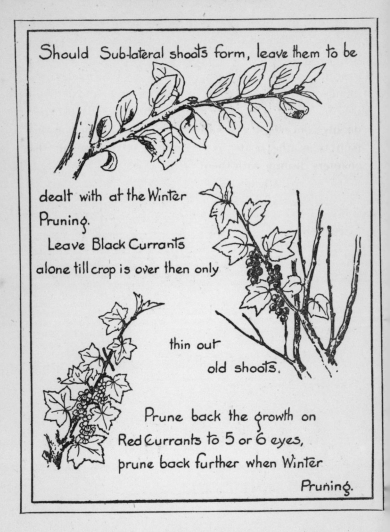

dealt with at the Winter
Pruning.
   Leave Black Currants
alone till crop is over then only

thin out
   old shoots.

   Prune back the growth on
Red Currants to 5 or 6 eyes,
prune back further when Winter
                              Pruning.

manent value, because they will be cut off at the winter pruning; therefore they must be "stopped" when one leaf, or at most two leaves, have developed. If summer pruning is practised earlier than at the times recommended the sub-laterals grow vigorously, and a good deal of labour is caused in pruning them. For further details concerning the summer pruning of the various fruit trees, the reader is recommended to consult the chapters dealing with them.

CHAPTER XVIII

Root Pruning

ONE always hesitates to recommend the root pruning of fruit trees because it seems such an unnatural sort of thing to do. Yet if a fruit tree persists in making vigorous unfruitful shoots, which become still more luxuriant the more severely they are pruned, and the room available for the development of the tree is limited, root pruning seems the only practicable thing to do.

I doubt if it is of much use so far as old-established trees are concerned; at all events, it is of far greater value in dealing with young trees. The object of root pruning is to prevent the trees from becoming filled with gross, unfruitful branches; that is a far better practice than first allowing them to make vigorous growth and then taking them up and cutting back the roots severely.

The kind of root pruning chiefly to be recommended is not concerned with cutting back old, thick roots, but with shortening those of recently planted trees. Most young fruit trees are likely to grow vigorously during the first few years after they are planted, and it should be the purpose of the grower to prevent their doing so.

It is not difficult to do this, providing the essential details are attended to regularly during the first three

An excellent Apple for amateurs—the cooking variety,
" Bismarck "

Fruit Trees
producing year after year
only gross, unfruitful
shoots need
Root Pruning.

they have probably
made coarse,
fibreless roots

Two or three year
old fruit trees growing
over luxuriantly can be
lifted, root pruned then
replanted to check growth & induce
fruitfulness

G

The way to mark out the site of trench, making use of a garden line tied to the bottom of the tree.

Take out the trench wide enough to work easily, and deep enough to expose the roots

Fork away the soil from the roots into the trench

or four years. All that is necessary is to take up the trees, a matter that is very easily done when they have been in the soil only for a year, shorten the thickest of the roots by half or so, and replant, taking care to cover the uppermost roots with only about three inches of soil. This kind of root pruning is a simple matter, and it is undoubtedly the best.

Sometimes it is thought necessary to root-prune large fruit trees that have been established for some years, yet do not bear fruits. But it is not likely to be of much avail unless the branches are kept well apart from each other and all superfluous shoots are cut out. Then it may be advantageous.

I have known old trees to be severely root-pruned and to suffer such a check to growth that they were almost killed; for two or three years they scarcely made any growth, and bore no fruits. Root pruning certainly did not pay, for if the old trees had been uprooted and young ones planted to replace them these would have proved far more profitable eventually. In dealing with large established trees it is a mistake to root-prune all the roots on one occasion. Those on one side of the tree ought to be pruned one year, and those on the opposite side the following year.

The way to proceed is to take out a trench two feet or so wide and of such a depth that it will be possible to get well underneath the roots. The soil must be forked away from the latter and placed outside the trench until all the thick, strong roots are exposed, search especially

Don't cut away fibrous roots if it can be avoided as these encourage fruitfulness

Work the soil from well under the tree in order to get at the tap root that is often the cause of most of the trouble

Make the cuts in this direction

and not like this

Endeavour to pull pruned
gross fibreless roots
into a horizontal position
to prevent their
growing again
straight down.

As the work proceeds
shield thin fibrous roots
with a mat or sacking to
prevent
drying,
before being again
covered with earth.
Mix loam, lime rubbish,
wood ashes etc with the soil
when filling in after pruning

being made for those right underneath that grow straight downwards. When found, they must be shortened to two or three feet. In replacing the soil, care ought to be taken to lay the roots in as nearly a horizontal direction as possible and to make the soil firm about them. The best time to carry out root pruning is late in October; in fact, as soon as most of the leaves have fallen from the branches.

CHAPTER XIX

Pruning Apple Trees

LET us first describe the orthodox pruning of an apple tree. There are five chief types of tree : the standard, which has a head of branches on a stem 5 feet to 6 feet high (the half standard is a similar tree on a shorter stem); the bush, which has a number of branches that arise near the base of the tree; the pyramid, which has a central stem from which branches grow throughout its full length; the cordon, which has one, two, or three stems, but no secondary branches, except the short side shoots on which the fruits are borne; and trained trees (dealt with in a separate chapter).

The orthodox method of pruning is much the same for all these forms of apple trees. It consists first of all in cutting out weakly and ill-placed shoots that tend to overcrowd and interfere with the development of the main branches; that process is known as thinning out, and is a necessary preliminary to the actual pruning or cutting back.

Then we come to deal with the main branches. Their pruning consists in shortening the part that grew during the previous summer by one-third, if they are only moderately strong, or by one-half, or even two-thirds, if they are rather weakly. Finally, there are the side shoots to be pruned.

Side shoots are those that develop on the main limbs of the tree and on which the fruits are borne. These are pruned twice a year—in late July or early August, and again in winter—during December or January. The summer pruning consists in shortening *the current summer's growth only* of the side shoots to within about six buds of the base; the older wood below that point must not be cut. In this connection it should be mentioned that the small leaves at the extreme base of the shoot are not to be counted. In the course of a few weeks further shoots will develop from the top of the shortened side shoots; these are known as sub-laterals, and should be cut off as soon as they have formed one or two leaves.

The Final Pruning

At the final pruning in December or January the side shoots are again shortened—this time to within two buds of the base of the past summer's growth. Thus the tree in winter will possess a limited number of main branches at from 12 to 18 inches apart, according to the kind of tree, and throughout the greater part of their length there will be shortened side shoots or spurs, which in the course of a few years become more or less gnarled and stunted as a result of the continued annual pruning on the lines described. Blossom buds develop on the spurs, and it is these that are relied on chiefly to produce a crop of fruit. Such is the orthodox pruning of apple trees as practised by gardeners, a method that

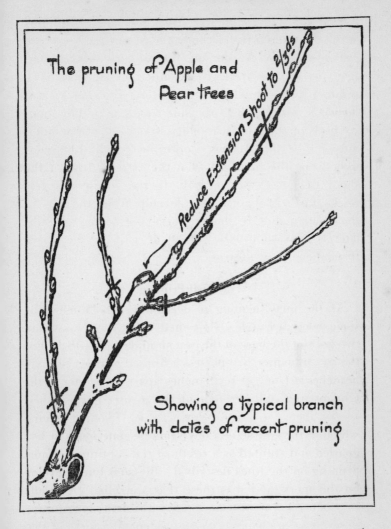

The pruning of Apple and Pear Trees

Reduce Extension Shoot to 2/3ds

Showing a typical branch with dates of recent pruning

has been in use for generations. But that is not the be-all and end-all of pruning.

Supposing that under this treatment the trees do not

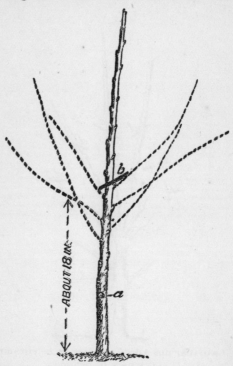

Maiden Apple tree; (*a*) where budded, (*b*) where
to prune. Dotted lines indicate fresh branches

bear satisfactory crops of fruit? That unfavourable *dénouement* may, of course, not be due to incorrect pruning : yet it is possible, even probable, that pruning has a good deal to do with it. For example, the trees may continue to produce strong, luxuriant branches on which blossom buds do not develop. In such a case root pruning may have to be undertaken to curb the excessive branch growth.

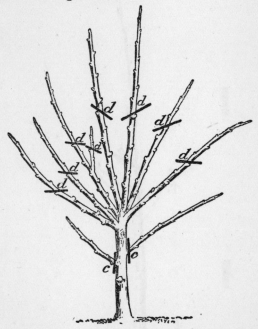

Two-year old Apple tree: (c) to be cut out,
(d) where to prune

The ground may have been over-manured with farm-yard or stable manure; if so, an application of basic slag in autumn and superphosphate of lime in spring will be beneficial. The tree may have been planted too deeply; if that is so, then it must be taken up in autumn

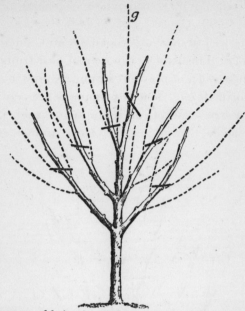

Two-year old Apple tree pruned to form pyramid:
(*g*) leading shoot. Dotted lines show future branches

and replanted with its uppermost roots near the surface.

Sooner or later amateurs will discover that all varieties of apples cannot be treated alike in the matter of pruning. That is the rock on which most inexperienced pruners come to grief. It is necessary to study not only the variety being dealt with, but the individual tree, so that it may be given exactly the kind of pruning it needs. Fruit trees grow differently in different gardens, so it is scarcely possible to lay down hard and fast rules. There are some that possess distinct characteristics, and these must be taken into consideration if success is to be achieved.

Take the well-known early cooking apple Golden Spire, for instance. This is one of those that bear fruits freely on the shoots of the previous summer's growth, therefore the orthodox method of pruning is scarcely suited to it. The tree must, of course, be kept shapely, and so the side shoots, that are likely to block up the centre of

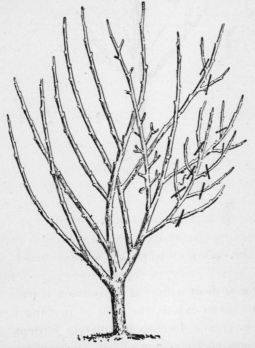

Bush Apple tree: (*e*) branch on which laterals have been pruned, (*f*) shows where to prune laterals

the tree and cause an overcrowded condition, must be shortened in summer and in winter as already described; but as the tree is of slender, upright growth it will be found possible to keep it in a fruitful state and shapely, chiefly by thinning out superfluous branches rather than by cutting them back severely. That method also answers well in pruning Bismarck, Margil, James Grieve, and Irish Peach.

The beginner must realise that the primary purpose of pruning is to induce the tree to bear fruit, and any method which does not bring about that condition is wrong. It is, for instance, of little avail to continue pruning a fruit tree in the orthodox way by cutting back the side shoots in summer and in winter if the result is not a yield of fruit; other methods must be tried.

Branches Must Not be Crowded

It will often be found that if the branches are kept well apart by thinning out those for which there is no room, fruit buds will form naturally and little summer and winter pruning will be required. A tree crowded with branches cannot bear good crops of fruit, and it is far better to cut some of them right out, letting in light and air, which will help the natural inclination of the tree to fruitfulness, than to continue cutting back the shoots and branches.

Providing that the general conditions are suitable— that soil, situation, and choice of variety are sound—I would say that apple trees are most likely to be made

Distinguish
between "leading" and
"side" shoots. the former
often require leaving

alone

Cut back side shoots to
within 5 or 6 leaves of
the base

and cut out entirely
any shoots attacked by blight
or disease and burn at once

fruitful by observing the following conditions. For the first three years after planting, the trees should be taken up in autumn, all long and thick roots then being shortened by half, and be re-planted immediately in unmanured soil with which lime rubble or mortar rubble has been mixed, if possible, the uppermost roots being kept near the surface. Let the branches be well apart from each other, say from 12 to 15 inches, according to the vigour of the variety and form of tree, and let all thin, weakly shoots, especially in the centre of the tree, be cut right out. Then it is likely that the orthodox summer and winter pruning will be very slight.

There is little doubt in my experience that the less one is obliged to prune an apple tree the better, and the greater likelihood there is of satisfactory crops. However, under artificial methods of cultivation, some pruning is necessary. When an old tree gets into the state that it makes such vigorous growth that the shoots and branches have to be pruned drastically annually, there is little hope for it. Either it is an unsatisfactory variety or the conditions of soil or situation are unsuited to it, and it were better to grub it up and plant another tree.

Cordon Pear trees on a garden wall

CHAPTER XX

Fruit Trees that require Special Pruning

THERE are innumerable varieties of apples in cultivation, and many show a marked variation in habit of growth, consequently correct pruning plays an important part in their management. If the trees are to obtain the maximum benefit each one must be treated according to its needs.

It is advisable to become familiar with both wood and fruit buds, so as to know exactly where to cut. There are two kinds of wood buds, the easiest to recognise being those on the current year's growth. These are situated in the axils of the leaves, are flattened in shape, and run out to a point at the tip. In the following season some remain dormant, others break forth into growth, which may either be long or short and terminate in another wood bud or fruit bud. It is this type of wood bud that is the most difficult to recognise, as it is round and plump like a fruit bud, the only difference being that it is more sharply pointed. In the following season these buds will be surrounded by a rosette of leaves, as with fruit buds, but the leaves will be fewer. On weak-growing trees it is almost impossible to distinguish between these wood buds and fruit buds, but in the spring following, the difference will be apparent.

H

Fruit buds form on one-year-old shoots in some varieties, but, as a rule, they take two seasons to develop. Understanding this, the pruner can work with a view to keeping his trees as far as possible correct in outline and the branches so arranged that light and air can reach all parts.

Severe Pruning not desirable

It should be kept in mind that while pruning is an essential cultural detail, it will not make barren trees fruitful, and if overdone it is liable to produce unfertile "wood." If trees show a tendency to make too much growth at the expense of fruit buds, it is often possible to correct them by simply "tipping" the leading shoots, instead of cutting them half-way back. In this chapter the remarks deal only with a few special varieties which need careful pruning, and we assume that the trees are well established and furnished with from six to ten main branches.

Pruning Popular Varieties

The popular varieties may be divided into three sets, viz., weak-growing, moderately vigorous, and vigorous. The first section includes such as Lane's Prince Albert, Gladstone, Grenadier, Early Victoria, Domino, and Stirling Castle. All these varieties—and there are several others similar in habit of growth—may produce fruit buds on the one-year-old wood, especially at the tips, which is a sure sign of a tendency to overcrop. For this reason the spurs should be thinned out occasionally, and when a well-balanced head of branches is secured, the leading shoots should not be shortened by more than one-half.

Summer Pruning

As to the general pruning, it should commence early in August, for the purpose of "stopping" such shoots as are very vigorous. There will not, however, be much tendency to overcrowding, and the chief item will be the prevention of over-cropping, on account of prolific fruit bud formation on both one and two-year-old wood. It goes against the grain to sacrifice the shoots that promise blossom, but the alternative, if the trees are to be kept healthy, is a severe thinning of the fruit when the season proves a good one. Lane's Prince Albert is characteristic of a few varieties that are of spreading habit of growth, and of which the branches are inclined to droop. To correct this tendency, prune in winter to a bud pointing upwards.

These need Careful Pruning

Apples of moderate vigour include the famous dessert varieties of Cox's Orange Pippin and James Grieve, and such favourite sorts as Lord Derby, Bismarck, Royal Jubilee, Potts' Seedling, Worcester Pearmain, and Allington Pippin. These are not quite so free in making natural spurs as the weak-growing sorts, especially on heavy land, and fruit buds are not produced so freely at the ends of lateral shoots that attain a length of from four to eight inches. At the winter pruning the leading shoots should be shortened by only about one-third; if too much growth follows, it is advisable to leave them practically full length for a season or two to prevent further luxuriant growth.

Pruning in Winter

When pruning the side shoots in winter, four or even five buds may be left instead of the usual two or three buds. Laterals so pruned will develop into unnaturally long spurs, which are not only unsightly, but take up more room than there is any need for. To prevent this, it is advisable to cut them out gradually at the winter pruning, as by the time this can be done sufficient natural spurs will have formed.

Pruning Vigorous Varieties

Among the vigorous apples are Bramley's Seedling, Warner's King, Gascoyne's Scarlet, Beauty of Bath, Lord Grosvenor, and Blenheim Orange. It is possible to prevent these varieties fruiting for a long time by too much pruning. While they are young, and the branches are being formed, a certain amount of hard cutting is essential, but in later years "tipping," or "stopping," the shoots in August, followed by cutting in winter to about half, is all that is needed.

Early Julyan and Domino are typical of a few varieties which may be said to be a class to themselves, for they retain their shape, despite remarkable freedom in the production of fruit buds on the year-old wood, which often makes hard pruning essential for the required new growth. Duchess of Oldenburg and Golden Spire are of very upright growth, and are useful to plant where space is limited. They generally need pruning lightly.

CHAPTER XXI

Pruning Pear Trees

AMATEURS will find little difficulty in pruning pear trees, for they are more uniform in growth than apple trees, and therefore require less discrimination in the use of the pruning knife. The grower who prunes his trees merely by the rule-of-thumb method, without exercising judgment, and without altering his system to suit the variety in question, will achieve greater success with pear than with apple trees; most of them are suited by the orthodox plan of summer and winter pruning already described in the chapter dealing with pruning apple trees.

Young pear trees usually grow very vigorously during the first few years after planting, and unless the precaution is taken to lift them annually in the autumn for the first three years and to shorten the thick roots they may before long become almost unmanageable, or, at least, such a thicket of growth that it will be difficult to bring them again into a fruit-bearing condition. The annual lifting and slight root-pruning ought to be considered essential, for it will be very difficult to regulate the growth of the young pear trees by branch-pruning only. If, however, their vigour is restricted in the way described while they are young they will gradually settle down, and once they begin to bear fruit crops with fair regularity this in itself assists in restricting the luxuriant growth of branches.

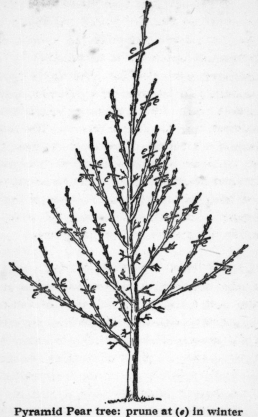

Pyramid Pear tree: prune at (s) in winter

Pear trees ought not to be planted in rich ground; no manure is required at planting time when the land is being prepared for them, but it may be put on the soil with advantage in early summer for the purpose of keeping the roots moist in hot weather.

In pruning standard pear trees the advice given in the chapter on pruning standard fruit trees should be followed, and for cordon pear trees the chapter dealing with this form of tree should be consulted.

The ordinary pear tree for planting in the open garden is usually in the form of a pyramid; that is to say, it has a main central stem on which branches develop almost from the base to the top. The pear tree is naturally of a pyramidal shape, and the form of tree known as a pyramid is the most suitable. The pear tree does not show nearly so much variation in manner of growth as the apple tree; some varieties of the latter make upright trees, others form rounded trees, while the branches of some are of drooping growth.

Orthodox Methods of Pruning

If the other details of cultivation referred to—annual lifting and root-pruning for the first few years and planting in suitable soil—are attended to, the orthodox method of summer and winter pruning will suit the pear tree. In July or early August the side shoots on the main branches are shortened to within about six leaves of the base of the current summer's growth, and in winter they are cut back farther to within two buds or so. That sounds very simple, and so indeed it is, but it is not quite enough.

cut off
side growths
from Cordon trees
at the
6th leaf
and from
shoots that form
again to 1 leaf as often as
produced.

Prune Cordon
Gooseberries also
by shortening the side shoots,
With Black Currants cut out
old Wood leaving young growth
to replace it.

The pear tree is a sun-lover, and unless the branches are kept well apart and the tree itself is in a sunny position, it may make a lot of growth, but fail to bear fruit freely. Above all things, see that all thin and weakly shoots inside the tree are cut right out in summer and winter so that the centre of the tree is open. Fresh

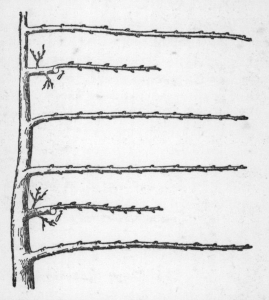

Old horizontal espalier of Pear; young shoots will grow if older, worn-out branches are cut as at (j)

shoots must not be allowed to grow at all unless it is intended that they shall develop into new branches for which there is room or unless they are to form fruit spurs and are pruned in summer and in winter; they should be cut right out before they have made much growth.

The aim of the pruner, not only in dealing with pear trees, but with all other fruit-trees, should be to obtain a tree with a limited number of main branches so wide apart that the fruit spurs on which blossom buds develop shall be open to the maximum of sunshine and air. Such treatment, combined with the usual process of summer and winter pruning, ought to produce satisfactory results, and is likely to do away with the necessity for severe cutting back, which is not to be recommended.

If the tree grows luxuriantly and bears little fruit it is not of much avail to continue cutting back the branches and shoots, for that will simply aggravate matters. The solution should rather be sought in thinning out, in root-pruning, and in correcting too rich a soil by the application of basic slag and superphosphate of lime instead of farmyard or stable manure.

CHAPTER XXII

Pruning Plum Trees

THERE are many plum trees in my garden, and I prune them very little indeed. In fact, some years I do not prune them at all beyond cutting out dead shoots or branches and any others that have exceeded the space allotted to them. I do not say that the trees are shapely; in fact I should be hard put to it to describe their form —certainly they do not come within the category of any standardised shape—they are really big bushes, but, and this is the main thing, they do bear fruit when the season is a favourable one.

How, then, does one prune plum trees? I do not think it is possible to lay down any hard-and-fast rules for pruning if one is to gather the maximum of fruit. Certain directions must, however, be observed. Important details are to plant them in soil that contains a lot of lime rubble, or old mortar rubble, to use no manure, to plant them with the uppermost roots just beneath the surface, and to lift and slightly root-prune them every year for the first three or four years after planting. In that way are laid the foundations of success, and the necessity of branch pruning is reduced to a minimum.

The growth of the trees must be regulated to some

Proper spur pruning
produces a large cluster
of fruit buds on a Plum tree.

a shoot left un-
pruned often produces
little more than
leaf buds

Cutting back of
side shoots to 2 or 3
buds being the
method adopted to induce the formation of fruiting spurs

Stop the side shoots
of Cordon Apples while in fruit
to 6 leaves from
the base

Raspberry Canes that have
fruited may be cut out, saving
this year's young canes.

Don't cut the natural Spurs of
Plum Trees: clusters of leaves
on short, stubby shoots with blossom buds
in the axils.

extent, of course, otherwise they will soon become a mere thicket. I advise the reader to thin out rather than to cut back. His trees will not be so shapely or such models of form as they might be, but in a "plum season" there is little doubt that he will have his share of fruit.

Keep the branches well apart from each other, 15 inches or so, cut out all dead shoots and weakly ones that tend to fill up the centre of the tree, cut away all suckers—those shoots that grow from the base of the tree—these are essential details.

As to the actual pruning of the branches, it is necessary to look over the trees in the summer for the purpose of cutting back any vigorous side shoots and to shorten them again in winter, but there will not be a great deal of this work to be done.

It is often advisable to let a young shoot grow to take the place of a weakly, dead, or ill-placed branch which it is desired to get rid of, for the plum bears fruit freely along its young shoots; that is to say those two or three years old, sometimes on those one year old. It bears also on spurs which develop naturally, and as the result of shortening the side shoots in summer and in winter. A good deal can be done in spring by disbudding; that is, by removing unwanted shoots while they are quite small. The check to the growth of the trees is reduced by following that method, and the need for pruning later on is lessened.

Don't be too particular concerning the shape of the plum trees; let them grow naturally, but take care to remove superfluous shoots while they are small and to thin out unwanted ones from time to time. This will save a good deal of cutting back, which is harmful and tends to give rise to the trouble known as "gumming." If large branches are cut out or much other severe cutting back is done, the chances are that "gum" will begin to exude from the branches, and if that happens the tree may go from bad to worse.

It may be worth while saying a word or two about the silver leaf disease of plums. Victoria is a very susceptible variety, so, too, is Pershore, but others are by no means immune. If a branch possessing the silvery leaves is noticed it ought to be cut out at once, and it is important that it should be burnt, because the disease spores spread from the dead wood. There is apparently no cure for this trouble, though cutting out affected branches immediately they are noticed and burning them may check it.

CHAPTER XXIII

Pruning Cherry Trees

MUCH of the advice given in the chapter dealing with plum trees applies also to cherry trees. They dislike being severely pruned, therefore it is wise to take such steps as will regulate the growth of the trees without using the knife. These are to plant in unmanured ground containing lime rubble, to lift the trees annually for the first few years (except in the cultivation of standards, which ought not to be disturbed), to use artificial manures rather than stable or farmyard manure, to keep the branches well apart from each other, and to thin out all superfluous shoots. There will naturally be a certain amount of summer and winter pruning of side shoots to be done to keep the trees fairly shapely, but it will be reduced to a minimum if the above advice is followed.

Cherry trees make admirable wall trees, and when they are grown in that way obviously more pruning is necessary than when they are planted in the open garden, but it should be done largely by disbudding in spring and pruning the green shoots in summer rather than by severe cutting back in winter. Young shoots can often be trained in to replace parts of old or decayed branches, and whenever that is possible it should be done.

The Morello cherry needs different treatment from the sweet cherries. It bears its fruits chiefly on short, slender shoots of the previous summer's growth, and in pruning the object is to cut out such old branches or parts of them as can be replaced by those of the past summer's growth. The pruning ought to be done as soon as the fruits have been gathered.

CHAPTER XXIV

Pruning the Peach and Nectarine

THESE fruit trees require exactly the same kind of pruning, therefore they are dealt with together; one is but a variety of the other. Peaches and nectarines are commonly grown against sunny walls in the milder parts of the country, though occasionally, in exceptionally favourable soils and situations, some varieties will thrive in the open garden. The method of pruning described applies to trees grown against a wall out of doors or on trellis under glass. Those grown as trees in the open are best suited by thinning out the superfluous shoots in spring so that the remaining ones are well apart from each other and are able to benefit by full exposure to air and sunlight, but few amateurs are able to attempt their cultivation in the open garden.

It must first be realised that the fruits of peach and nectarine are borne chiefly by the shoots or branches of the previous year's growth, therefore important details are to cut out the old branches as soon as the fruits have been gathered and to train the new ones to the wall in place of them, as reliance must be placed on the latter for the following year's crop.

Another detail of equal importance is disbudding. This must be attended to carefully or the shape of the trees will soon be spoilt, the branches will be crowded and the trees will be worthless. Disbudding, which is done in spring, consists in removing many of the young

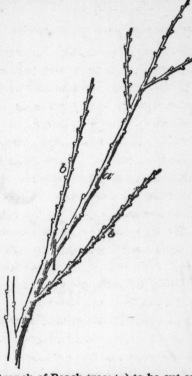

Branch of Peach tree: (*a*) to be cut out in early autumn, (*b*, *b*) to be tied in

shoots or growths when they are an inch or so long. They are usually very numerous on the branches, and if all were allowed to remain and reach full size the tree

Be careful not to shake off fruits when pruning as often happens when the knife is blunt.

For Peaches, shoot bearing this year's fruit to be removed.

this year's shoots left to bear fruit next year

With Raspberries, cut away the old canes and tie in the new.

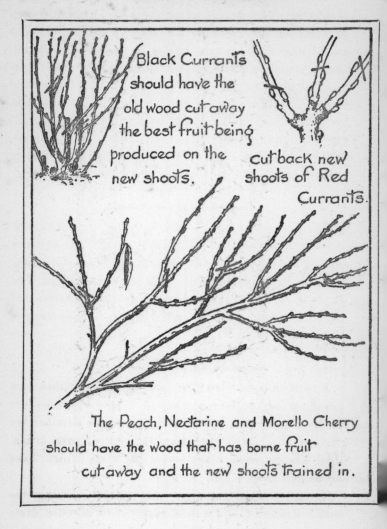

Black Currants should have the old wood cut away the best fruit being produced on the new shoots.

Cut back new shoots of Red Currants.

The Peach, Nectarine and Morello Cherry should have the wood that has borne fruit cut away and the new shoots trained in.

would be a thicket of growth. When disbudding is finished not more than two or three of the fresh shoots ought to remain on each of the old branches. One of these must be as close to the base of it as possible and another must be at the top; a third shoot somewhere near the middle of the branch may be left if there is room for it to be trained in to form still another branch, but if there is no room, then only two fresh shoots are left on each old branch, one at the top and another somewhere near the base.

Take Care of New Shoots

The purpose of the shoot at the base of the old branch is to provide a new one, which at the end of the summer will be as long as the old one, and will replace it when, the fruit having been gathered, the latter is cut out. The shoot left at the top of the branch is for the purpose of ensuring a supply of sap for the proper development of the fruits.

Branches Renewed every Year

It will thus be seen that most of the branches of a peach or nectarine tree that is treated correctly are renewed every year. Those that grow one summer are cut out in a year's time after they have borne fruits, their places being taken by a fresh set which have developed meanwhile.

These new shoots grow very rapidly during the summer months, and it is necessary to tie them securely but lightly alongside the branches they will replace; they will then fit in the spaces previously occupied by the old branches, and when the time comes to tie or to nail them in there will be little difficulty in retaining the shape and symmetry of the tree. If, however, they are allowed to become misshapen during the summer it will be difficult so to arrange them as to make a presentable tree. Thin secondary growths often develop on the summer shoots, but they are of no value and ought to be cut right out.

Training Peach and Nectarine

The branches of the peach or nectarine are trained in the shape of a fan at about five inches or so from each other, the lowest branches being horizontal and the remainder gradually rising until, in a well-preserved and well-developed tree, they almost meet at the top, the last branches being, of course, almost upright.

Disbudding is Important

Many gardeners take a great pride in their peach and nectarine trees, which are models of perfect form and accurate training. Unless care is taken to select a new shoot as near the base of the old branch as possible the chances are that the tree will become bare at the base and in the centre. The young shoots must be removed gradually, a few at a time throughout a period of three weeks or so. To remove so much foliage at one time might be prejudicial to the progress of the tree. The shoots on the upper part of the tree should be thinned out first, those on the lowest branches being dealt with last of all. Peach and nectarine trees are naturally apt to get bare towards the base and it should be the aim of the grower to prevent this as far as possible by retaining young shoots low down.

CHAPTER XXV

Pruning Raspberry, Loganberry, and Blackberry

IT is scarcely possible to go wrong in pruning the summer-fruiting raspberry. The fruits are produced by the canes that grew during the previous summer, therefore when the year's crop has been gathered the old canes are cut out and the new ones are tied to the support to replace them. Could anything be simpler? In spring more fresh shoots usually grow from the base of the raspberry than are wanted, and it is important to remove those for which room cannot be found, while they are small, so that the remaining ones may have the chance to make vigorous growth. Not more than five or six canes are left at each clump. In the spring it is usual to look over the raspberry canes and to cut off the tips if they are soft and very thin or have been damaged in winter. Otherwise there is no further pruning to be done.

Certain varieties of raspberry bear fruits in late summer and early autumn, and are known as autumn-fruiting raspberries. These need pruning differently from the ordinary summer-fruiting sorts.

In the spring—February is a suitable time—all the canes are cut down to within 5 or 6 inches of the ground level; the result is that the plants are forced to send up a number of vigorous canes or stems that will bear fruit

Cut out old
canes of Logan
and Raspberries
& leave the new.

Cutting down
newly planted
canes to about 6"
will induce 2 strong suckers
to be thrown up.

This method of pruning Raspberries to various heights induces
them to fruit near the ground, with
stronger canes & larger fruit

in September and October. It will thus be seen that while summer-fruiting raspberries bear their fruits on the stems of the past summer's growth the autumn-fruiting kinds fruit on the stems of the current year's development.

During recent years many varieties of berried fruits similar in growth to the blackberry and loganberry have been introduced to gardens; they have proved very valuable, for they are easily grown and rarely fail to bear satisfactory crops. Their pruning is carried out in exactly the same way as advised for the summer-fruiting raspberry, for the fruits are borne by the stems or branches that grew during the previous summer.

As soon as the fruits have been gathered all the old canes should be cut right out and the new ones tied to the support to replace them and to bear the following year's crop. It is necessary to limit the number of new shoots in spring for they are usually numerous, and room cannot be found for all of them.

These new shoots are rather a nuisance during early summer, but they must be taken care of, for we have to rely on them for the following year's crop. Perhaps the best way of dealing with them is to tie them loosely to the older branches until the latter have been cut out after the fruit-gathering. All the various berried fruits— Lowberry, Himalayan Berry, Laxtonberry, and others— are pruned in the same way.

CHAPTER XXVI

Pruning Gooseberry Bushes

THE first thing the grower should endeavour to do is to prevent overcrowding of the branches; if that is accomplished, then there is every likelihood of good crops of fruit being obtained. If pruning is neglected, the bushes will certainly become full of shoots which will not bear fruits, and will effectually prevent others from doing so.

The branches ought to be so far apart that the hand can be passed down between them conveniently; in other words, they will have to be ten inches or so from each other. In an ideal gooseberry bush there should be a limited number of main branches well covered with fruit spurs, the space between them being entirely free of other shoots. The method therefore recommended is that of thinning out rather than of severe pruning.

Cut out all superfluous shoots for which no room can be found, but without interfering with the development of such a bush as has just been described. Then fruit spurs will form naturally in numbers, and others can be induced to do so by shortening the side shoots in summer and cutting them back to two buds or so in winter. The leading shoots, those at the ends of the branches, should be slightly shortened in winter, but not cut hard back, unless, of course, the bush has filled its allotted space; they will often bear fruit the following year.

Some varieties of gooseberries are naturally of drooping habit of growth; their branches may drag on the ground, and then any fruit they bear will probably be

Pruning young Gooseberry bush: (*f*) where to prune, (*g*) growth on stem to be cut off

spoilt. Branches that are so near the ground should be cut off; the bush should have a stem clear of very low branches so that the soil beneath can be cultivated properly during the summer months. Otherwise weeds will flourish there. In pruning the branches of varieties that are of drooping habit, it is wise to cut to buds that point upwards, as this helps to some extent to correct the drooping habit of growth.

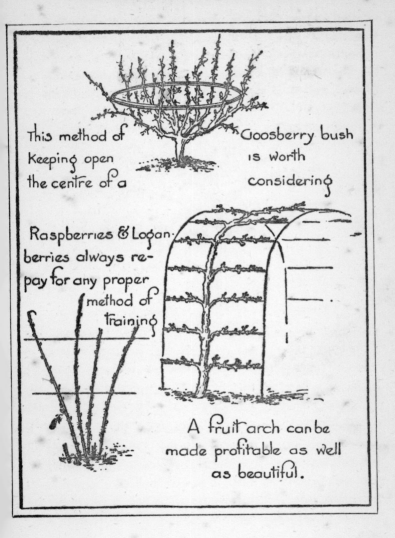

This method of
Keeping open
the centre of a
Goosberry bush
is worth
considering

Raspberries & Logan-
berries always re-
pay for any proper
method of
training

A fruit arch can be
made profitable as well
as beautiful.

Gooseberry trees are often grown in the form of cordons, either for planting against a wall or against a trellis in the open garden. In that form it is essential to prune them in the orthodox way by shortening the side shoots in summer and cutting them in winter to within one or two buds of the base of the previous summer's growth. This is known as spurring back. The

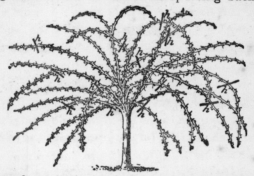

Gooseberry bush of drooping growth: prune at (h)

leading shoots, those at the ends of the branches, are allowed to grow unchecked during summer, and in winter are shortened by about one half. Gooseberry trees in this form are well suited to amateurs' gardens, for they are very easily managed, and as a rule the fruits are finer than on bushes, though they are not so abundant.

CHAPTER XXVII

Pruning Currant Bushes

AMATEURS are likely to experience little difficulty in pruning currant bushes, for the matter is really a simple one. The first thing to know is that red and white currant bushes are pruned in a similar way, and that the black currant needs quite different treatment.

The fruits of red and white currants are produced chiefly by spurs—short woody branches that develop as a result of continued annual summer and winter pruning of the side shoots. In July the latter are pinched or cut off at about the sixth leaf, and in winter they are cut back to within half an inch or so of the base of the previous summer's growth.

It is necessary to keep the branches well apart from each other by thinning out unwanted shoots so that the spurs on the branches are open to sunshine and air. Crowded bushes are not likely to be satisfactory. The aim should be to have a limited number of main branches at 9 or 10 inches apart and to have these covered with fruit spurs for the greater part of their length. This result can be obtained only by preventing overcrowding, by cutting out shoots for which there is no room, and pruning the side shoots in summer and winter in the way already described.

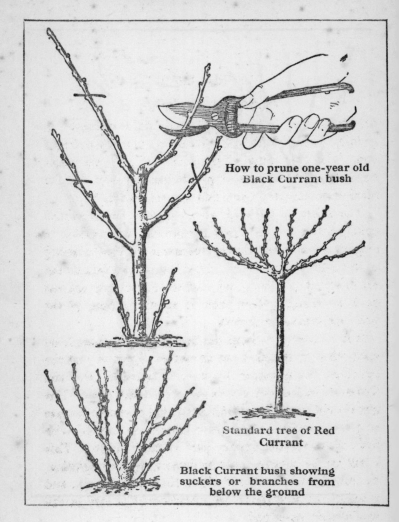

How to prune one-year old
Black Currant bush

Standard tree of Red
Currant

Black Currant bush showing
suckers or branches from
below the ground

In the case of
Black Currants
cut out old wood
mainly & retain
strong young
shoots

Cut back side shoots
of Red & White Currants
to 2 or 3 buds and shorten the
leaders by about half

.Make the cut close
above an
outward pointing
bud, or in the
direction you wish the
future shoot to grow.

As the fruits of the black currant are borne chiefly by the branches of the previous summer's growth, it is

The uppermost illustration shows a pruned
Red Currant bush: the lower, a trained tree
pruned

obvious that a different method of pruning is necessary. The best time to do the work is as soon as the fruits have been gathered in late summer. The way to prune is to cut out such old branches as can be replaced by others of the past summer's growth. The object should be to have as many of the past summer's shoots in the bush as possible and to get rid of older wood to make room for them.

Very often the young shoot develops in such a way that only part of the old branch can be cut out, for it is obvious that the latter can be shortened only to the point at which the new shoot arose. The same instruction as to keeping the branches well apart from each other holds good; overcrowding is certain to bring unsatisfactory results.

Big bud or black currant mite, which is the bane of growers of this fruit, is less likely to cause serious harm if the old wood is cut out regularly and burnt than if pruning is neglected.

CHAPTER XXVIII

Pruning Apricot, Medlar, Mulberry, and Nut

APRICOT trees are usually trained in the shape of a fan. Two of the most reliable varieties—Moorpark and Shipley—bear their fruits chiefly on spurs two and three years old, but other varieties bear fruit mainly on the shoots of the previous year's growth. With all varieties summer pruning and disbudding are essential. In May all shoots that are ill-placed and growing out practically at right angles to the main branches should be rubbed off, reserving the thin, wiry shoots that can be conveniently nailed to the wall or tied in for next year's fruiting. In July vigorous shoots should be "stopped"; they will eventually form fruit spurs.

In dealing with apricot trees it is always wise to bear in mind the advantage of allowing young shoots to develop for the purpose eventually of replacing older ones, for these are liable to die off in an unaccountable fashion; in any case, it is wise to cut out old branches occasionally if they can be replaced by young ones. Refurnishing the apricot periodically with new branches contributes largely to the continued healthfulness of the tree, but it must be a gradual process : cutting out large branches generally leads to disaster.

Winter pruning is best done before the turn of the year. Cut out parts of the branches of four year's standing when they are beginning to look bare, if there are young shoots to train in their places. Shorten the previous summer's growth to a point where it seems to be thoroughly firm; in dealing with very weak shoots, cut them harder. At the extreme ends of the branches always leave a growth, not only for extension, but to act as a sap conductor. With the Moorpark apricot bear in mind the need for the production of fruit spurs and retain the small lateral shoots, which in some varieties would be an unnecessary encumbrance.

Pruning the Mulberry

Mulberries are fruits of easy cultivation, and will succeed admirably where the soil is not too clayey. The fruit is borne on short-jointed young wood and on spurs, vigorous shoots as a rule being unfruitful. The trees may be trained as standards or bushes; in the former pruning is chiefly a matter of cutting out shoots where there is any overcrowding, and removing weak shoots from the centre. It is when grown on walls and fences that systematic pruning is required, and most of it is best done in summer by removing or "stopping" the grosser shoots, so as to expose the branches to light and air. The weaker shoots, which, if retained full length, would lead to overcrowding, should be "stopped," thus encouraging the formation of spurs. If proper attention is paid during summer there will only be superfluous shoots here and there to remove in winter and any spurs which have proved barren.

Medlars are generally budded on pear stocks, and their pruning is very similar to that required by the pear. Summer pruning is advisable to prevent overcrowding and to strengthen the buds that remain. The removal of such shoots as appear superfluous may be done in early summer, but August is soon enough to take the points out of side shoots that are to be retained. In winter cut back the side shoots to three or four buds, shorten the leading shoots by about half, and cut out the weak growth that always develops near the centre as this is seldom fruitful.

Cob and filbert nuts are worth a place in every garden, for they are very fruitful if a little attention is paid to their training. After the single stem has been made to branch about two feet from the ground pruning is best done when the blossoms have faded in February. The fruit is produced on well ripened but thin shoots of the previous year's growth. The male blossom is the well-known catkin, but the female resembles a minute brush, and is of pinkish colour. Every twig carrying the female blooms must be retained, as there is always an abundance of catkin-bearing wood that can be cut out. This should be removed to admit plenty of light and air to the centre of the bush; any strong shoots which it may be thought advisable to retain for future branches should be shortened by about half. The chief thing is to keep the centres of the bushes open, and all suckers—shoots that grow from the soil level—must be removed.

CHAPTER XXIX

Pruning the Vine

MANY amateurs possess glasshouses in which they attempt the cultivation of the vine with varying success. It is probably true to say that most of the failures are due to an insufficient knowledge of pruning : at all events, this has an important bearing on the matter, for correct pruning is an essential detail of the management.

Before attempting to prune a fruit tree it is wise to find out how the fruit is borne, otherwise we may do a great deal more harm than good. Grapes are produced by the summer's growth, which arises directly from buds that developed on the previous year's shoots. As our purpose is to induce vigorous growth that will bear large bunches of grapes we shorten the previous summer's shoots to within one or two buds of the base in winter, when the vine is dormant. We allow the vine to grow freely throughout the summer, and then in winter, when all the leaves have fallen, we cut back those long, strong shoots until only one or two buds remain. That seems a strange, and indeed a wanton, thing to do, but the purpose is sound and the result is satisfactory.

In the first place, there would be no room for all the shoots that developed during the summer, even if we wished to leave them; and, secondly, the shoots would be weakly and overcrowded to such an extent that the grapes would have no chance of developing, let alone ripening. By cutting back each of last year's branches to within one or two buds of where it started to grow we concentrate the energy of the tree and force it to produce a limited number of vigorous shoots.

All the side branches that grow at intervals on the main stem are treated in this way. If there is still room for the vine stem to extend, the leading shoot may be left from 18 to 24 inches long; when the vine stem reaches the top of the glasshouse the leading shoot must also be pruned back to one or two buds.

In spring the vine will start into growth, and then disbudding has to be done. If both the buds left on each of the side branches start to grow, one of them must be rubbed off, but before that is done we must decide which of them is to be preferred. One of them may possess an embryo bunch of grapes, the other may not; in that event we naturally let the former remain and rub off the latter. If there is a bunch of grapes, this can be distinguished when the shoot is only an inch or two long. If neither shoot has a bunch, and one is stronger than the other, we should keep the stronger and remove the other. Only one fresh shoot must be allowed to develop at each spur—a spur is the gnarled and woody growth that results from the continued annual pruning of the side branches.

During summer the new shoots grow very quickly, and soon the bunches of grapes will be clearly distin-

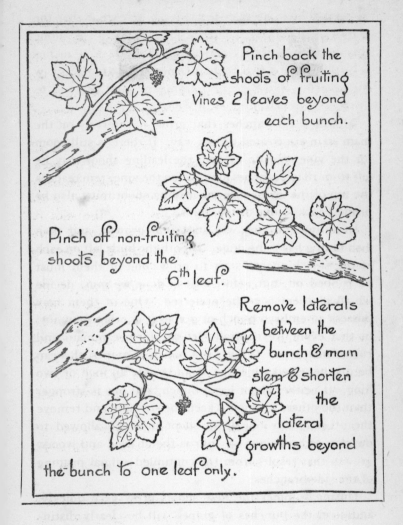

Pinch back the shoots of fruiting Vines 2 leaves beyond each bunch.

Pinch off non-fruiting shoots beyond the 6th leaf.

Remove laterals between the bunch & main stem & shorten the lateral growths beyond the bunch to one leaf only.

guishable. If we allow these shoots to grow unchecked they will soon smother the trellis, with the result that the developing grapes will be deprived of light and air and probably fail to ripen. So, when the shoots are 15 inches or so long, we pinch off or cut off the ends. If they bear grapes we "stop" each shoot just beyond the second leaf above the bunch.

It is unwise to carry out this summer pruning all in one day. Let the work extend over a week or more, cutting a few shoots each day. If it is done properly we shall then have a vine which possesses one or more stems, and issuing from the "spurs" on either side of the stem there will be these green shoots, many of them bearing grapes, and each shoot shortened in the way described.

What happens next? The uppermost buds on the side shoots will start to grow, and will give rise to other smaller growths, which are known as sub-laterals : they must be "stopped" when they have made one, or at the most two, leaves. In this way we shall force the vine to concentrate its energies on producing a limited number of large leaves on the lower part of the shoot and good quality grapes.

By winter the side shoots will have become hard and woody, and we must cut them right back to within one or two buds of where they started to grow in the previous spring.

Those who plant a young vine which consists of one stem only should allow it to progress up the trellis at the rate of not more than two feet each year. The stem may reach almost to the top of the trellis at the end of the first summer, but, even so, in winter it must be cut down to within two feet of where it started to grow, and the same procedure must be followed every year, until the top of the trellis is reached.

As the vine stem increases in length its buds will start into growth, and we rely on the shoots they produce to bear the grapes. There will be many more shoots than we can find room for, so some of them must be rubbed off while they are small. Those allowed to remain should be about 18 inches apart, those on one side alternating with those on the opposite side as far as can possibly be managed. At any rate, they ought not to be opposite one another.

We have to remember that the first side shoots are the beginnings of the spurs on which we shall rely in future years for the fruit-bearing shoots. It is therefore worth while taking trouble to select those that are conveniently placed.

PART III

PRUNING TREES AND SHRUBS

CHAPTER XXX

Some General Directions

THE correct pruning of trees and shrubs can be carried out only by those who have some knowledge of their habit of growth, flowering season, and other characters. In the absence of such knowledge more harm than good may be done.

The following may be cited as the four chief objects or main reasons for pruning trees and shrubs.

1. To develop a well-balanced and shapely tree or shrub, having in view its distinctive habit of growth and the position in which it is growing.

2. To improve the quality of the blossoms and to ensure a satisfactory display of them.

3. To aid in maintaining health and vigour.

4. The periodical removal of dead wood from old trees to keep them attractive as long as possible.

Opponents of pruning, and they do exist, may point to the natural beauty of a wood which, they say, is never visited by man with a chopper or saw. Such trees, planted fairly close together, hold one another up, as it were, and in the main keep a good leader. Looked at *en masse* the effect may be very good, but commence to examine each tree in detail and it will be found that the number of good specimens is not large.

The good effect of pruning is even more marked amongst shrubs. There is no comparison between two shrubbery borders, the one systematically pruned, the other allowed to grow at will; the coarse, strong-growing shrubs—which should only provide shelter and a setting for the choice ones—overcrowd and spoil the beauty of rare and less vigorous kinds.

It is possible to over-prune trees and shrubs, and thus to destroy their characteristic growth. A collection of trees and shrubs would be robbed of half its beauty and interest if all were pruned in exactly the same way to approximately the same shape and height.

Much harm is often done when the garden is "spring-cleaned" in February or March. Off come the shoots of the Mock Orange (Philadelphus), the Forsythia, the Diervilla (Weigela), and the Kerria, to say nothing of the Clematis montana on the house. Is it any wonder that the owner of a small garden decides to root out the shrubs because they do not flower freely? The correct time to prune these shrubs is immediately after flowering, not a short time before they should bloom.

Those who love their gardens and find in gardening the most engrossing and healthy of all recreations will discover that the subject of pruning—how, when, and why to do this or that—among the most interesting of garden "operations."

The term pruning is used here in its broadest sense, especially with regard to deciduous-flowering shrubs. It includes not only the shortening of branches and twigs, but thinning out the branches—the removal of the old branches to make way for young ones, and limiting the number of new shoots, the object being to throw the vigour into a limited number, and thus to obtain better growth and flowers. Obviously, if the number of branches on a tree is regulated so that light, air, and sun reach them the growth must be vastly improved. With certain kinds of trees the pruning and thinning of branches is done chiefly while they are young. Too much stress cannot be laid on the necessity of a good beginning. Many flowering shrubs require pruning more or less throughout their lives.

It is obvious that the old practice of doing all the pruning required in a garden during one or two weeks when tidying up the beds and borders as winter gives place to spring is entirely wrong. A large number of trees and shrubs require no regular pruning, but it is fairly safe to say that all trees and shrubs during their early years of growth benefit by at least a little thinning of the shoots, shortening of the branches, or training of the leading shoot. It is a great mistake to neglect pruning for five years or more and then have a real good "set-to." A considerable number of flowering shrubs only give the best results when they are pruned or the growths are freely thinned annually.

In a garden of fair size the pruning of trees and shrubs

Laden with blossom in spring—the double white Cherry

may be said to be more or less continuous throughout the year. Certain kinds are best pruned in winter or during early spring, others which include the Forsythia, the Philadelph.., and Kerria, should be pruned and thinned as soon as the flowers fade.

Though these remarks point to the necessity of pruning being done with considerable thought and care, as the grower becomes familiar with the various trees and shrubs cultivated, he will find the art of correct pruning and thinning no more difficult than, and quite as interesting as, other phases of gardening.

Pruning should begin while trees and shrubs are young. Neglect to pinch off a few shoots with the thumb and finger may in later years mean sawing off large branches.

K

CHAPTER XXXI

Pruning Trees

THE pruning of large-growing trees is deserving of much more attention and consideration by cultivators. Too often they are planted and left to grow without any thought of what they will be like in ten, twenty, or more years. Close planting tends to the development of tall, slender growth, with the leader drawn upwards in the struggle for light. This is a condition favoured by growers of timber, as the lower branches fall away when young, leaving no knots or scars in the wood. In planting ornamental trees ample space must be allowed for their development. The general tendency of isolated trees is to develop laterally rather than in an upright direction.

To obtain good specimen trees, with stately trunks and well-balanced branches, pruning should commence when the trees are young. The beginning in the nursery usually consists of pinching out the points, and cutting out small shoots to give ample space for the selected few to develop. It is a common practice to cut off the lower branches to form a clean trunk quickly, but a much better result is obtained by leaving a few side branches to feather the trunk for a few years. If these are kept rather closely pruned they help materially in the development of the trunk, but do not increase much in size, so that when cut off there are only comparatively small wounds to heal over.

Early thinning and training of young trees should do away with the necessity for the removal of large branches in later years. Equally important is it to remember that a tree with well-balanced branches is less likely to suffer damage during gales.

In pruning, do not attempt to destroy the individuality of a tree. The tulip tree, the maidenhair tree, and the false acacia (Robinia) are naturally more or less upright in growth. Consider, when pruning, what a contrast these provide in the pleasure grounds to the wide-spreading Catalpa, the horse-chestnut, and the manna ash (Fraxinus Ornus).

One of the first and most important considerations is the training of a healthy growth as the central or leading shoot of the tree. This is destined to become the trunk in later years. Having selected the healthiest and most convenient central shoot, all rival growths should be shortened, or entirely removed. Young trees supported with stakes may at times, especially when leafless, look unnatural, but as stakes may make just the difference eventually between a crooked and a straight trunk, their temporary support must be looked upon as essential.

Sometimes a leader develops an unusual length in one season, and has no side branches. Matters can be balanced by shortening the shoot to half or even one-third its length. This will cause the development of several other growths, the best one of which can be selected to become the new leader of the tree, the others being "topped" when perhaps six inches long, or entirely removed if there are too many.

A common mistake is to leave a considerable number of branches on the larger growing trees when young. Remember that the side branches continue to produce their quota of new shoots each year, and will eventually become very large, requiring ample space for development. The remedy is to remove those branches not required, but it necessitates leaving a wound on the main trunk. If, however, the cut is made with care, and dressed with tar, the wound will eventually completely heal over on healthy trees.

Occasionally the leader of a tree may be broken or damaged by accident. On deciduous trees a suitable side growth near the top can usually be found to tie in position as a new leader. If one is not available for the time being, cut the broken shoot clean out and await the development of a new one.

The majority of specimen trees growing in an open position do not attain their normal height unless the growth of the side branches is checked. By encouraging the development of the leading shoot and regulating the development of the side branches, trees are encouraged to attain their normal maximum height.

Some trees naturally fork or divide into several main branches low down on the trunk. It may be taken as a good general rule to encourage the development of a single trunk to a good height. Not only is it more imposing, but it is not unlikely that in a gale one of several large limbs on a low-forked tree, which in time become excessively heavy, may break off.

An enthusiast coming into possession of a long-neglected garden probably finds numerous trees which have been left unpruned for years. Severe treatment is necessary, though the trees may look rather disfigured for a year or two.

When to Prune

From the foregoing remarks it will be apparent that the main business of pruning and thinning the growths of trees is the encouragement of certain selected branches, and the checking or suppression of others to build up evenly well-balanced specimens.

The pruning of young and old trees may be carried on during eight months of the year. The four months when pruning is not desirable are February, March, April, and May. During this period the sap is very active, and many trees "bleed" freely if the wounds made by pruning are of any size. Birch, walnut, the Prunus family, and maple, are among the most susceptible.

Pollarded and Coppiced Trees

In pollarding, the young branches are cut back to a desired height, usually about 10 feet or thereabouts. The willow is the tree most frequently pollarded. Coppiced trees in woods, and willows in damp ground, are cut down to the base. How often the branches are cut down depends on the size of the stakes required. Close coppice planting and cutting encourage the growth of straight poles. Ash, hazel, sweet chestnut, and willow are the trees most frequently coppiced. The young willow rods are cut every year for basket-making. The sweet chestnut poles are split and used extensively for light fencing.

In meadows and park-land used for grazing it is necessary to remove the lower branches of trees to prevent damage by cattle. Nothing looks much worse than a tree with its lowest branches leafless and damaged.

Street Trees

In most positions where street trees are planted limited space necessitates much closer pruning and shortening of branches than is normally practised on trees growing in pleasure grounds and parks. The choice of trees suitable for street planting is limited, though it must be admitted that the London Plane is far too often planted. It is, however, certainly the best tree to withstand injury from the city smoke, and can be pruned more or less indiscriminately.

Street trees must have more than usually tall trunks; branches low down would interfere with traffic and pedestrians. When trees are allowed to grow tall in narrow roads, those in charge may expect to receive complaints from residents that the trees are obstructing light from the rooms, and probably making it impossible to grow flowering plants satisfactorily in the front garden. This means that the top, bottom, and sides of the trees have to be severely limited. Then follows the hard pruning often so severely criticised; but is there an alternative? When once the close framework of branches is formed, thinning and shortening, if done in alternate years, tends to keep the trees within bounds.

Under natural conditions of growth, without pruning, trees become crowded with branches. When some of these are cut out, dormant or latent buds often produce numerous small growths, which must be removed. The common lime is one of the worst offenders in this respect; if left unpruned a tangled mass of thin, twiggy growths develops on the trunk. When this is cleared out there is usually an annual or biennial crop of other shoots to remove. It saves a lot of bother from this cause when clean cuts are made close back to the branches.

Pruning Hedges

No hard-and-fast rules are made with regard to the best times to prune hedges. The practice varies very considerably with the different shrubs planted as hedges, and the time selected for clipping or pruning may also be a matter of local convenience.

When such closely clipped evergreen hedges as holly, yew, and box are pruned once only during the year this is best done in late summer, August, when growth for the year is practically completed. In town and suburban gardens owners intent on keeping their privet hedges neat and tidy clip them from May to August at intervals of four to six weeks. In bygone days our predecessors, who took so much pride in their topiary work, clipped their yew, box, and holly hedges quite as frequently.

In country gardens there is nothing to equal the quick or thorn hedge when this is closely clipped. It forms a very neat and impenetrable hedge when clipped twice during the season—in June and again during August.

It is practically impossible to prevent a hedge from increasing a little in size each year. Then there comes a time when hard pruning is necessary; perhaps once in five years, or oftener, the secateurs, or even a small pruning saw, must be brought into use, and the shoots are cut well back into the hard wood. April is the best time for the drastic pruning of laurel, privet, holly, yew, evergreen oak, and other similar hedges. Though it probably means losing a season's flowers, April is also the best time to prune rhododendrons and the large-leaved evergreen bushes severely.

Some shrubs cultivated for their flowers as well as the leaves are best pruned after flowering. Good examples are Escallonia, Berberis stenophylla, Berberis Darwinii and Cydonia japonica.

Tall hedges of beech, hornbeam, or cherry plum can be kept neat by annual pruning with shears in late summer.

CHAPTER XXXII

Pruning Conifers

THE pruning of conifers, or cone-bearing trees, differs in several ways from the pruning of flowering trees. If, from any cause, owing to an accident, or its destruction by insects, the leading shoot of the tree is destroyed, it is useless to tie up the nearest suitable side branch to form a new leader.

In abies and picea, for example, which are of very formal outline, with a well-defined central stem, the branches develop in more or less regular whorls or tiers. It is useless to tie up one of these side branches with the idea of forming a new leader, for it will grow one-sided and very slowly. The procedure necessary to obtain a new leader is to cut out the remains of the damaged one, then, usually near the top, one or more new shoots will push out from dormant or latent buds. The most suitable one can be selected for a new leader and the others removed.

The growth of thuya, cupressus, and tsuga, is different. In pruning these it is often necessary to shorten the numerous upright-growing side branches, which develop as potential rivals to the proper leader.

Care is necessary in shortening the side branches of abies, picea, and similar conifers. Always shorten close to a side branch or twig, making the pruning as little apparent as possible, for they have not the power to make new growth rapidly and recover, as have most flowering trees.

Half-dead branches, i.e., branches with many dead twigs near the bottom of the tree, should be cut clean out to the trunk; that is a better practice than merely cutting out the dead parts in the hope that they will recover.

Because of the large amount of resin and other substances in the wood of conifers, pruning should, as far as possible, be done in late summer, autumn, and early winter, when the flow of sap, at least in developed trees, is not at its height. Though dressing of wounds with tar is to be recommended, there is little likelihood of disease attacking them, because the sap is in itself somewhat antiseptic; the sap possesses preservative qualities, for it is well known that the wood and branches of conifers do not decay readily.

CHAPTER XXXIII

Tree-Pruning Troubles Solved

WHEN the pruning and thinning of trees has been carefully and systematically undertaken until they are of fair size, with a well-grown trunk, they may be left more or less to develop their natural shape and characteristic features. There are, however, exceptional circumstances. Something unforeseen may happen, such as damage by winds, certain branches may become unsafe, or it may be necessary to open up a view; in such conditions large branches have to be removed sometimes.

The dying back of old trees, oak trees in particular, is a subject which the expert is asked to explain from time to time, and to suggest suitable treatment. The most probable cause usually is that the tree has absorbed a large proportion of the available plant food in the area covered by the roots, and, having attained its maximum development, it is unable to "pump up," as it were, sufficient nourishment to reach to the ends of all the branches.

The best treatment is to cut off the dead and unhealthy ends of the branches, pruning back to sound wood; to loosen the surface soil over the whole area under the tree, and just beyond the spread of the branches, and to apply a dressing of turfy loam with which decayed manure and such useful fertilisers as bone meal, wood ashes, and soot, have been mixed.

When it becomes necessary to remove large branches, always endeavour to do the work in the autumn or early winter; October and November are the best months, when plant life is least active.

In practice it is found that there are two distinct types—soft and hard woods—with, of course, many intermediates. Examples of half a dozen soft wood trees are birch, horse chestnut, lime, prunus, some acers, and many of the conifers. Only cut large branches off these trees in late autumn and winter when it is absolutely necessary, and then dress the wounds with tar immediately. The best examples of hard wood trees are the oak, elm, hornbeam, ash, and plane. These can be pruned with safety from the beginning of June until the end of January.

Always cut off a branch close back to the main trunk or to a healthy side branch, leaving no vestige of a snag or stump. When a piece is left on, if only a few inches long, it must inevitably die, as there is no growth at the end to draw up the sap. The dying back not only occurs at the end, but the decay extends right back into the main trunk or branch, causing a hole. When, however, the cut is made close to the main branch, it gives new bark a chance to grow gradually over the wound, especially on young, healthy trees, and, in fact, all those in full vigour. An elm tree can almost always be relied upon to push out vigorous new growths the following season when stumps are left after pruning; so, too, can the plane.

Large branches should be removed in several pieces. The last piece cut off ought not to be very long, or in falling its weight may carry away a strip of bark from the trunk, or from the larger branch to which it is attached. To safeguard against this, cut through several inches of the bark and wood at the bottom with upward cuts before sawing through from the top. As an additional precaution, fasten heavy pieces of wood to a branch above with a rope so that the branch will remain slung in position when cut right through.

Too much stress cannot be placed on the desirability, one may even say the necessity, of making perfectly clean cuts and dressing the wounds or cut surfaces with an antiseptic. Various substances have been used, and are recommended from time to time—Stockholm tar, creosote, and styptic, or carpenter's knotting—but none equals coal tar from the gasworks — not the tar mixtures used as a surface dressing for roads, for they contain additional substances. Coal tar is at once an antiseptic dressing against fungous spores and a protective coating of the wood against the weather.

The practice of protecting large wounds by nailing on sheets of tin, zinc, or lead is wrong. What a splendid harbour or refuge they provide for insect and fungoid pests ! All that is necessary is to renew the dressing or coating of tar when required, not more than once a year, until the new bark grows over and completely covers the wound. Only dress the cut surfaces, not the living bark, with tar.

Small cuts at the ends of branches are often passed over as not sufficiently important to dress with tar, but it is desirable to coat the cut end of branches the size of one's finger and larger, especially if the tree is a "soft wood"—prunus, birch, or magnolia, for instance. The deadly coral spot fungus (Nectria cinnabarina) frequently starts on small branches, gradually working back, so that first of all branches die, and eventually the whole tree or bush perishes.

Insufficient attention is, as a rule, given to the removal of branches on large trees. Not only on the score of tidiness in appearance, but also for the general health of the trees, the latter should be looked over periodically for the purpose of cutting out dead wood.

The pruning of evergreen trees differs a little from that of deciduous trees. For example, the shortening, thinning, and general regulation of the branches is best done when new growth is about to begin in spring. The chief reason for this is that the sap is more or less active throughout the year, thus if pruning is done in autumn the tree will attempt to make new growth, which will be checked or possibly killed by frosts in winter. It is important to remove superfluous shoots and wrongly placed growths while they are small.

Holly and yew are attractive trees for the lawn when only sufficient thinning and pruning of the branches is done to allow of the development of a pleasing outline.

CHAPTER XXXIV

Pruning Shrubs

In the management of such a very large and varied collection of hardy shrubs as we now cultivate in our gardens, it is not surprising that the methods of pruning are diverse. Many shrubs do not require pruning, in fact, are better without it, the magnolia, for example, but in practice it is found desirable to prune most shrubs at some period or other to make them suitable to the positions occupied, or to improve their shape.

The time of flowering provides a fairly reliable guide as to the best time for pruning. Many shrubs flower on the current season's shoots, the remainder blossom on the shoots of the previous year. The second group is very much the larger and more important, and the flowers are produced chiefly during the first half of the year; in dealing with these, whatever pruning of shoots and thinning of branches is required should be done when the flowers fade, to allow as long a season of growth for the new shoots as possible. Six well-known shrubs that need this kind of pruning are Forsythia suspensa, Prunus triloba flore pleno, Clematis montana, Kerria japonica flore pleno, Philadelphus Lemoinei erectus, and Deutzia gracilis.

Shrubs that blossom on the wood or growths of the

current year should be pruned between November and
the end of February. Good instances of shrubs that need
this treatment are Hydrangea paniculata grandiflora,
Spiræa japonica, "Anthony Waterer," Buddleia variabilis, Hypericum Henryi, Ceanothus Gloire de Versailles,
and Clematis Jackmanii. During the development of
the young shrubs only moderately hard pruning may
be necessary, but when they have attained the required
size the previous year's growths may be cut back to
within a few buds of the older wood. The harder the
pruning, the stronger will be the new growths and the
better the flowers.

A large number of flowering shrubs need thinning
rather than pruning; superfluous shoots or branches are
cut out so that those remaining may have space to
develop, and that light and air may penetrate into the
bushes. The spring-flowering spiræas—among them
S. arguta and S. Thunbergii—most of the mock oranges
(Philadelphus), the shrubby honeysuckles, the Diervilla
or Weigela, and the Escallonia, may be cited as examples.

Shrubs which give a certain amount of trouble in
pruning are those cultivated for their attractive fruits.
Notable examples are some of the barberries, the wild
roses, pyracantha, and the cotoneasters. If these are
pruned in winter, or early spring, the bushes will probably produce few if any flowers, hence there can be no
hope of a good display of fruits. If pruning is done
after flowering, this removes the small fruits that are
developing.

Flowers of the Golden Bell shrub. (Forsythia spectabilis.)

Probably the best thing is to do a little thinning and shaping of the bushes in June, and about every fifth year to prune hard in early spring. This means the loss of a season's flowers and fruits, but instead there should be an abundance of vigorous new shoots to carry on the healthy life of the bushes.

In pruning and thinning shrubbery borders the bushes must be restricted to their allotted space. When the routine methods are not sufficient to keep them within bounds, the pruning necessary to prevent the bushes outgrowing their positions is usually best done in spring, before new growth for the year begins.

There comes a time when shrubs which require no regular pruning either outgrow their positions or become very dense, unshapely, or overgrown. This calls for a vigorous cutting back of the old branches with a corresponding thinning and shortening of the remainder. The large-leaved evergreen rhododendron provides one of the best examples. It means the loss of a year's flowers, but it is wonderful how soon a rhododendron bush recovers, provided, of course, that a fairly good foundation of stems exists to which the branches can be shortened, the older worn-out wood being removed down to the base if need be.

April is the best time to cut back old rhododendron, laurel, privet, and phillyrea bushes. The old cut stems may look ugly for a week or two, but dress them with tar immediately after pruning, and in a few weeks there should be a good crop of young growths.

L

Pruning Evergreens

When evergreen bushes are cultivated entirely or for the most part for their foliage, spring as a rule is the best time for pruning. Just when new growth is about to begin is found to be the most satisfactory season, whether for cutting the stems hard back into the old wood because the shrubs have outgrown their space, or if it is simply a matter of shortening some of the longer branches to ensure shapely bushes.

It is worth while also to go round with the sécateurs during August when growth for the season is practically completed, shortening, or removing entirely, vigorous new shoots which may in time spoil the appearance of a bush or lead to its outgrowing the space available. When such work is neglected for a year or two it is surprising how soon a shrubbery border becomes a mass of tangled growths.

Useful foliage effects can be obtained by severe annual pruning of, among other shrubs, Ailanthus glandulosa, Paulownia imperialis, and Rhus typhina var. laciniata. If cut down to the ground each year in early spring the shrubs produce very vigorous shoots with large handsome leaves. When each plant is limited to one stem quite a tropical effect can be obtained.

Pruning Climbers and Shrubs Grown as Climbers

The pruning of climbing plants, and shrubs cultivated as climbers, is one of the most important details of their cultivation. Practically all climbers require some pruning and training in order to keep them within bounds and to adapt the growths to whatever support it is intended they should cover.

A number, we will take the clematis and climbing roses as examples, flower very much better when pruned and thinned annually so that there is a frequent supply of young wood to produce plenty of blossoms.

In the case of shrubby plants grown against walls and fences, a good deal of pruning and training is necessary to change their habit of growth from bushy shrubs to upright growing plants for the purpose of furnishing walls, fences, and other supports. Hence it will be readily understood why we must prune a shrub considerably when it is planted against a wall, yet in the open border little pruning, if any, might be required. It is a case of adapting the plants to conditions rather than pruning to increase the supply of flowers, though incidentally many such plants bloom better against a wall, presumably because they obtain shelter and the growths are better "ripened."

In a garden with one or two sheltered walls numerous shrubs that are scarcely hardy can be successfully grown even though they are not climbers in the strict sense of the word.   Good examples are the myrtle, pomegranate, and crinodendron.

APPENDIX

Trees and Shrubs to Prune in Winter

NUMBERS of trees and shrubs require pruning before new growth commences in spring, some time between November and the end of February.

Ailanthus glandulosa.—The "Tree of Heaven" develops very large handsome leaves when the stems are cut down to within six inches of the ground each year in February and only one strong shoot is allowed to grow.

Berberis.—The leaf-losing Barberries require no regular pruning, but the bushes should be kept fairly thin and open by cutting out a few of the oldest stems in winter.

Buddleia variabilis.—This Buddleia produces the best flower spikes when hard pruned; cut the growths of the previous summer back to within one or two buds of the base in January or February.

Calluna (Ling).—No pruning is usually required, but when grown in formal beds long uneven shoots should be cut off in February.

Caryopteris.—The ends of thin growths are usually cut by frosts. Prune back to firm wood in February. This makes a good dwarf bush if the stems are cut down annually in early spring.

Catalpa.—The Indian Bean tree requires no regular pruning but the trees are low and spreading unless, when young, the branches are shortened to make them grow upwards.

Ceanothus.—The late summer and autumn flowering sorts flower best when rather hard pruned. When grown as bushes cut strong shoots of the previous summer's growth back to a length of nine to twelve inches, shorten the weaker shoots to one or two buds and cut out thin wood not required. On a wall or fence cut back the secondary shoots to within a few buds of the main branches.

Clematis.—Varieties that bloom in July and later, those of the Jackmanni and viticella types, are pruned in spring, the shoots of the previous summer's growth being cut down to within 10 to 12 inches of the base. These varieties of Clematis bloom on the fresh shoots of the current year's growth. Those that flower in spring and early summer, varieties of the lanuginosa, azurae and other types, must not be pruned severely: it is sufficient to cut out very crowded or thin, weakly shoots in winter or early spring.

Colutea (Bladder Senna).—Prune the young growths of the previous year fairly hard in February, especially in dealing with plants on walls and fences.

Corylus (Nut).—The varieties with coloured leaves give the best effects when the old stems are cut down.

Eccremocarpus scaber.—The stems of this climber often die back in winter. In cold districts they may be killed to the ground. Cut back to where the stems are alive or to the ground if there is no life remaining in the stems.

Fuchsia.—The branches are often killed in winter and must be cut down to the ground in February. In pruning Fuchsias on walls cut back the branches to new shoots just developing, in April.

Hydrangea paniculata and the variety *grandiflora* give the best display when the previous year's growths are shortened to within one or two buds of the old wood in February. Thin the new shoots about two months later as they are usually crowded.

Hypericum.—The St. John's Wort (*H. calycinum*) gives the best results when cut back to within three or four inches of the ground annually during February or early March. When the bushes become crowded cut out the older wood from the taller growing Hypericums early in the new year, and shorten the previous year's growth to within an inch or two of the main stems.

Jasminum officinale (White Jasmine).—Keep the plants thinned by cutting out old or very weak growths.

Juglans.—The Walnuts are unsatisfactory trees to prune. They seem to be overflowing with sap and "bleed" profusely when cut. Though no regular pruning is required, if any thinning or shortening of the branches is contemplated do the work in early winter when plant life is at its lowest ebb.

Laburnum.—No pruning desirable. If any shortening of branches is proposed in small gardens, do this in February.

Leycesteria formosa (Pheasant Berry).—In February thin crowded bushes by cutting out some of the oldest wood and remove all weak, thin, twiggy shoots. Also shorten ends of long branches.

Lippia citriodora (Lemon Scented Verbena).—On a wall or fence tie in long growths required to furnish the available space and prune back all secondary shoots to within a bud or two of the main branches in February. In bushes the vigorous shoots should be shortened and weak ones cut out at the same time. If the ends of the shoots have been killed prune back to firm wood.

Lupinus arboreus (Tree Lupin).—Cut out old worn-out wood and weak branches in February. Then cut the previous year's growths back to firm wood—it may be necessary to shorten them by half.

Olearia Haastii (New Zealand Daisy Bush).—When the bushes are young the ends of the shoots should be removed occasionally. When the bushes become overgrown, cut the large branches back into the old wood from which young shoots grow readily.

Passiflora coerulea (Passion Flower).—Tie in young shoots required then shorten long trailing growths to within two or three buds of the main branches.

Pernettya mucronata.—No definite pruning, but in February or March look over the bushes, shortening a growth here and there to keep them shapely.

Prunus.—Most of the flowering Cherries, Peaches, Plums, etc., need no systematic pruning. Some time during the winter look over them and cut out thin crowded twigs and shorten extra long branches that destroy the balance of the trees.

Pyrus.—No definite system of pruning is required, but there is a considerable amount of thinning of branches and twigs to do. Most of the Pyrus are best cultivated with a trunk and central main shoot from which the branches radiate. The secondary branches should be cut back or thinned to let light and air into the centres of the trees.

Rhus typhina (Sumach).—The best method is to restrict each plant to one stem and cut this down to within a bud or two of the base each year in February.

Rosa (Rose). — The wild Roses flower and fruit best when allowed to grow naturally, just thinning the bushes and cutting out old wood when necessary. Should a bush become old and "leggy" cut it down to within one foot of the base, at the end of February.

Sambucus (Elder).—The Golden Elder is the only one much grown; it should be cut back to within one or two buds of the old wood annually in February.

Spiraea.—In this large and valuable family of hardy shrubs there are two distinct sections : (1) those flowering in spring and early summer; (2) those flowering from mid-summer onwards. It is the second group that needs most pruning. In pruning *Spiraea japonica*, *salicifolia*, *Douglasii*, and *Menziesii* the old and weak wood should be cut down to the ground in February, leaving sufficient vigorous healthy growths. Shorten the latter to varying lengths of from one foot to about three feet. In pruning the tall growing Spiraeas *arborea*, *Aitchisonii*, and *Lindleyana*, shorten the secondary growths to within four inches of the main branches.

Symphoricarpus (Snowberry).—When the beauty of the white fruits is over cut out the oldest stems. Also chop round the outsides of the clumps with a spade to prevent their spreading.

Tamarix pentandra (Tamarisk).—The previous year's growths are cut back during February to within a few buds of the old wood.

Tecoma (Bignonia).—Both the kinds, *radicans* and *grandiflora,* are vigorous climbers for warm, sunny walls. Cut back the secondary shoots in February to within two or three buds of the base.

Viburnum.—The leaf-losing kinds require no regular pruning, but old wood can be cut out and long shoots shortened in April.

Vitis (Vine).—Vines on walls and verandahs should be cut back to one or two buds of the main branches in December. Once or twice also during the summer Vine shoots should be shortened.

Wistaria.—The previous summer's growths should be shortened to within two or three buds of the old wood in winter. The best display of flowers is produced on trees with plenty of short spur-like wood.

Trees and Shrubs to Prune in Spring

MOST of the shrubs which are improved by spring pruning can be placed in one of two groups : (*a*) Those which blossom in winter and early spring; and (*b*) Ornamental Evergreen Shrubs which are best pruned about April, just previous to the development of new growths.

Aucuba.—One of the best evergreen shrubs for town gardens, stands almost unlimited pruning and thinning.

Buxus (Box).—No regular pruning, bushes and hedges growing too large may be fairly hard pruned in April. Clip Box edging at the end of April.

Chimonanthus fragrans (Winter Sweet).—Bushes in the open require no regular pruning; a little thinning may be desirable after flowering. When growing on a wall or fence spur back the shoots after the flowers fade.

Choisya ternata.—Prune in April to make the bushes shapely. When grown on a wall some shortening of the shoots is necessary in spring and again later in the year.

Cornus Spaethii.—When cultivated for its beautiful red stems in addition to the attractive golden yellow foliage cut the old stems down to the ground in March.

Cotoneaster.—The evergreen sorts need no regular pruning, but it is often necessary to shorten long shoots to maintain shapely bushes.

Cydonia.—Bushes may need a few growths shortened and some thinning of the branches when very thick. If grown as a hedge, pruning with secateurs should be done after flowering. Secondary growths on wall plants should be cut back to within a few buds of the main branches.

Forsythia.—Shorten the longest of the shoots each year after flowering. The slender shoots of F. suspensa should be cut fairly hard back each year when the flowers fade.

Hamamelis (Witch Hazel).—No pruning required. When

the bush is young it may be necessary to shorten a long growth or two.

Hedera Helix (Ivy).—Ivies on walls and fences should be cut close back with shears annually in March. In August look over the walls and fences again and cut off loose or straggling new growths.

Hibiscus (Althæa) syriacus.—No regular pruning required, but crowded bushes may be thinned in April.

Jasminum nudiflorum.—The Winter Jasmine gives the best results when the shoots are cut back to within three or four inches of the main branches after flowering.

Laurel (Prunus Laurocerasus).—Hard pruning of hedges and bushes, if required, is best done during April. Shortening the summer growths is desirable in August. The Portugal Laurel (*Prunus lusitanica*) thrives under similar treatment.

Laurus nobilis (Bay).—If fairly hard pruning is essential it should be done in April. Closely cut specimens may be cut with a sharp knife or secateurs two or three times from June to September.

Lavandula (Lavender).—When Lavender hedges or bushes become overgrown cut them fairly hard back into the old wood during April.

Mahonia Aquifolium (Mahonia).—This beautiful evergreen shrub flowers from February to April. After flowering, do any pruning necessary to shape and thin the bushes. When planted as an undergrowth it should be cut over in April each year.

Myrtus (Myrtle).—Plants growing against walls or fences must be kept within bounds by shortening long branches in April each year. Bushes in the open and in tubs require a little shaping by shortening long branches about the same time.

Polygonum baldschuanicum.—Cut off all loose and superfluous growths during February if the plant has outgrown its space.

Prunus triloba flore pleno and *Prunus japonica flore pleno* flower best when the branches are shortened to within two or three buds of the old wood as soon as the flowers fade.

Punica (The Pomegranate).—When grown in a warm position as a bush the Pomegranate requires no regular pruning. If there are any long growths shorten them in April. This is also the best time to cut back the secondary growths on the main branches of trees against a wall or fence.

Pyracantha.—Bushes in the open need no definite pruning; in spring shorten branches that spoil their shape. When planted against walls or fences considerable annual pruning is desirable in April; cut back shoots that have grown too far from the support. It is better to do a little pruning each year rather than adopt drastic pruning once every four or five years.

Rhododendron.—April is the best month to cut back severely, old, overgrown bushes. Also, in April, remove the points of young plants to make them bushy.

Rosmarinus (Rosemary).—Requires no regular pruning, but towards the end of April cut off long ends of shoots to shape the bush and clip hedges of Rosemary. Trim long shoots again in early August.

Rubus (Brambles).—In spring when the strong, new shoots commence to grow from the base cut down all the old stems of the "Whitewash" Brambles : R. *biflorus*, R. *giraldianus*, R. *lasiostylus*, etc.

Ruscus (Butcher's Broom).—Remove the oldest stems in spring.

Salix.—Dwarf Willows cultivated for their bright red or yellow stems in winter should be cut hard back to within one or two buds of the old wood in March each year.

Spartium junceum (The Spanish Broom).—Shorten the growths freely when young to lay a good foundation of stems. Shorten the shoots annually early in April.

Syringa (Lilac). — Old and unhealthy Lilac bushes can often be given a new lease of life if the long straggling branches are removed in April, cutting well back into the old stems.

Veronica (Shrubby Speedwell).—These beautiful flowering shrubs only require pruning when the bushes outgrow their positions or become tall and bare at the base. When this happens they will break freely from the old stems if cut down by about half.

Viburnum Tinus (Laurustinus.—Prune little or much during April, as needed.

Trees and Shrubs to Prune in Summer

VERY little hard pruning is necessary or desirable in summer. It is primarily a season of thinning out weak and crowded growths, removing old branches that have blossomed and shortening excessively long shoots which would spoil the shape of trees or shrubs.

Abelia.—Cut back old branches to strong new growths; when stems get worn out cut them down to the base. Cut out weak twiggy wood when growths become crowded.

Amelanchier.—No regular pruning, thin out crowded branches in early summer after flowering. In pruning the dwarf, bushy variety oblongifolia several of the oldest stems should be cut out down to the ground to encourage the development of suckers from the base.

Azara.—No regular pruning, shorten long, bare branches in early summer after flowering.

Azalea.—No regular pruning but thin bushes by cutting out an old branch or two after flowering.

Berberis.—Prune the evergreen Barberries after flowering, when thinning or shortening of the branches is required. Cut back hedges of *B. stenophylla* and *B. Darwinii* immediately after flowering and trim again four or five weeks later.

Buddleia globosa.—Shorten long branches after flowering, to keep the bushes close and shapely. Cut off thin straggling ends of branches on bushes of *Buddleia alternifolia* immediately after flowering.

Buxus.—Box hedges and Box trees used for topiary work may be cut twice or three times during the summer with shears.

Ceanothus.—The spring-flowering kinds, when grown as bushes, require no definite pruning, just keep them open and shapely. Those on walls and fences should be pruned, the side shoots being cut back to within two or three buds of the main branches after flowering.

Cistus.—No regular pruning. Cut off old flowers and any very long shoots to keep the bushes shapely.

Clematis.—Prune spring-flowering sorts in early summer. Cut off the straggling growths of *C. patens* and *C. florida* varieties after blooming.

Crataegus.—The Thorns are not the easiest of shrubs to prune. If large branches are cut off big trees the wounds seldom heal satisfactorily, hence thinning and branch regulation should be done when the trees are young. There is always a certain amount of thinning to be done—July is the best time.

Cytisus (Broom).—It is necessary to prune young plants of Broom to form a good foundation, otherwise they soon become tall, leggy bushes. The longest shoots of older plants should be shortened when the blooms have faded, but do not cut back into the old wood as this does not produce useful new growths.

Deutzia.—Cut several of the oldest branches down to the ground each summer, to encourage strong young growths which produce the best flowers.

Diervilla (Weigela). — Each year after blooming cut the secondary or flowering twigs back to strong young shoots which, as a rule, are fairly numerous. Cut out old, worn-out branches.

Erica.—Prune the spring flowering Heaths lightly after flowering. The dwarf kinds may be cut back with shears when they are used as an edging. *E. carnea* and the variety *alba* in particular thrive and flower freely under this treatment. The tall growing kinds are apt to become straggling unless the longest shoots are shortened after flowering.

Escallonia.—On walls and fences shorten the shoots well back after flowering. Should one or two growths attain excessive vigour take out the tops or remove them entirely. In mild districts Escallonia hedges are cut with shears after flowering though it is preferable to use secateurs.

Euonymus.—When planted as hedges or formal bushes cut once or twice in summer as required. *E. radicans* planted as a carpet beneath trees should be cut over during July. If it is used as an edging to beds or borders clip with shears late in June and again during August.

Genista.—When young, shorten the growths two or three times in summer to prevent the bushes becoming "leggy." Afterwards they need no regular pruning; long shoots may be shortened after flowering.

Helianthemum.—Cut off the faded blooms and trim back straggling shoots.

Hydrangea Hortensia.—Remove the old blooms when they fade. Cut out very old wood and thin the weakly shoots, but only slightly shorten the strong young shoots as these produce the best flower heads the following year. Cut off the old flower heads of the climbing Hydrangea *petiolaris* (*scandens*) in late summer.

Ilex (Holly).—Clip Holly hedges early in August. During July or August shape Holly trees and bushes on lawns or in beds and borders by cutting back long shoots with secateurs. If it is intended to cut Holly bushes or hedges hard back into the old wood it should be done in late April.

Kerria japonica.—Cut out the old stems when the blooms fade.

Lavandula (Lavender).—Cut back the plants to just below the flowering spikes when these fade in August and generally trim and tidy the bushes.

Ligustrum (Privet).—To keep the hedges of Privet tidy and shapely clip them several times during the summer at about monthly intervals.

Lonicera (Honeysuckle).—When climbing Honeysuckles have ample space to grow over arbours, etc., they need no regular pruning, but old blooms and long ends of loose shoots should be cut off after flowering. Once in every four or five years a good thinning out of old stems may be desirable. Bush honeysuckles require no regular pruning, but after flowering cut out old worn-out branches.

Magnolia.—The only safe pruning is to shorten the longest shoots slightly after flowering to keep the bushes shapely. Long shoots of Magnolia on walls should be shortened to keep them shapely. The branches of Magnolia grandiflora may be thinned and regulated in April or early May, tying in only the best healthy shoots.

Philadelphus (Mock Orange).—About midsummer or as soon as the flowers fade cut out some of the oldest stems. Sometimes these can be removed to the ground, more often only to where there are vigorous young shoots. Some of them, notably *Lemoinei erectus*, *purpureo-maculatus*, and

Virginale produce a profusion of strong annual growths when all the stems are pruned, some to the ground, others back to vigorous young shoots on the main stems.

Rhododendron.—Remove old flower heads when the blooms fade. At the same time shorten long and remove crowded growths.

Ribes (Flowering Currant).—Cut out old wood and weak twigs after the bushes have flowered.

Spiraea.—After flowering look over the bushes of the spring and early summer blooming Spiraeas and thin out old and weak wood where crowded. Do this to the following Spiraeas during May and June immediately after flowering; *arguta*, *prunifolia flore plemo*, *Henryi*, *Wilsonii*, *canescens*, *media*, *Van Houttei*, and *Thunbergii*.

Syringa (Lilac).—After flowering look over the bushes removing the old blooms and weak young growths.

Aim to have a limited number of vigorous shoots which will produce flowers the following year. Remove sucker growths.

Ulex (Gorse).—After the main display of flowers is over, shorten the longest branches. After about ten years the plants will probably become straggling, when the bushes will stand cutting back into the hard wood early in April, say to within about two feet of the ground.

Wistaria.—Shorten the young shoots to five or six leaves in July and again shorten the secondary growths in August.

INDEX

PART I

Pruning Rose Trees

PART II

Pruning Fruit Trees

PART III

Pruning Trees and Shrubs